T0185112

Lecture Notes in Computer Science   11520

Commenced Publication in 1973
Founding and Former Series Editors:
Gerhard Goos, Juris Hartmanis, and Jan van Leeuwen

More information about this series at http://www.springer.com/series/7409

Tao Zhang · Jinpeng Wei ·
Liang-Jie Zhang (Eds.)

Edge Computing –
EDGE 2019

Third International Conference
Held as Part of the Services Conference Federation, SCF 2019
San Diego, CA, USA, June 25–30, 2019
Proceedings

 Springer

Editors
Tao Zhang
Cisco Systems
Iselin, NJ, USA

Jinpeng Wei ⓘ
University of North Carolina
Charlotte, NC, USA

Liang-Jie Zhang ⓘ
Kingdee International Software Group
Co., Ltd.
Shenzhen, China

ISSN 0302-9743   ISSN 1611-3349 (electronic)
Lecture Notes in Computer Science
ISBN 978-3-030-23373-0   ISBN 978-3-030-23374-7 (eBook)
https://doi.org/10.1007/978-3-030-23374-7

LNCS Sublibrary: SL3 – Information Systems and Applications, incl. Internet/Web, and HCI

This Springer imprint is published by the registered company Springer Nature Switzerland AG
The registered company address is: Gewerbestrasse 11, 6330 Cham, Switzerland

Preface

The aim of the International Conference on Edge Computing (EDGE) is to become a prime international forum for researchers and industry practitioners alike to exchange the latest fundamental advances in the state of the art and practice of edge computing, identify emerging research topics, and define the future of edge computing.

EDGE 2019 was part of the Services Conference Federation (SCF). SCF 2019 had the following ten collocated service-oriented sister conferences: 2019 International Conference on Web Services (ICWS 2019), 2019 International Conference on Cloud Computing (CLOUD 2019), 2019 International Conference on Services Computing (SCC 2019), 2019 International Congress on Big Data (BigData 2019), 2019 International Conference on AI & Mobile Services (AIMS 2019), 2019 World Congress on Services (SERVICES 2019), 2019 International Congress on Internet of Things (ICIOT 2019), 2019 International Conference on Cognitive Computing (ICCC 2019), 2019 International Conference on Edge Computing (EDGE 2019), and 2019 International Conference on Blockchain (ICBC 2019). As the founding member of SCF, the First International Conference on Web Services (ICWS) was held in June 2003 in Las Vegas, USA. The First International Conference on Web Services – Europe 2003 (ICWS-Europe 2003) was held in Germany in October 2003. ICWS-Europe 2003 was an extended event of the 2003 International Conference on Web Services (ICWS 2003) in Europe. In 2004, ICWS-Europe was changed to the European Conference on Web Services (ECOWS), which was held in Erfurt, Germany. To celebrate its 16th birthday, SCF 2018 was held successfully in Seattle, USA.

This volume presents the accepted papers for the 2019 International Conference on Edge Computing (EDGE 2019), held in San Diego, USA, during June 25–30, 2019. EDGE 2019 puts its focus on the state of the art and practice of edge computing, in which topics covered localized resource sharing and connections with the cloud. We accepted six papers. Each was reviewed and selected by at least three independent members of the EDGE 2019 international Program Committee. We are pleased to thank the authors, whose submissions and participation made this conference possible. We also want to express our thanks to the Organizing Committee and Program Committee members, for their dedication in helping to organize the conference and in reviewing the submissions. We would like to thank Prof. Teruo Higashino, who provided continuous support for this conference. We look forward to your great contributions as a volunteer, author, and conference participant for the fast-growing worldwide services innovations community.

May 2019

Tao Zhang
Jinpeng Wei
Liang-Jie Zhang

Organization

General Chair

Teruo Higashino   Osaka University, Japan

Program Chairs

Tao Zhang   Cisco Systems, USA
Jinpeng Wei   University of North Carolina at Charlotte, USA

Services Conference Federation (SCF 2019)

SCF 2019 General Chairs

Calton Pu   Georgia Tech, USA
Wu Chou   Essenlix Corporation, USA
Ali Arsanjani   8x8 Cloud Communications, USA

SCF 2019 Program Chair

Liang-Jie Zhang   Kingdee International Software Group Co., Ltd., China

SCF 2019 Finance Chair

Min Luo   Services Society, USA

SCF 2019 Industry Exhibit and International Affairs Chair

Zhixiong Chen   Mercy College, USA

SCF 2019 Operations Committee

Huan Chen   Kingdee International Software Group Co., Ltd., China
Jing Zeng   Kingdee International Software Group Co., Ltd., China
Liping Deng   Kingdee International Software Group Co., Ltd., China
Yishuang Ning   Tsinghua University, China
Sheng He   Tsinghua University, China

SCF 2019 Steering Committee

Calton Pu (Co-chair)   Georgia Tech, USA
Liang-Jie Zhang (Co-chair)   Kingdee International Software Group Co., Ltd., China

EDGE 2019 Program Committee

Zesheng Chen	Purdue University Fort Wayne, USA
Nicola Dragoni	Technical University of Denmark, Denmark
Maria Gorlatova	Duke University, USA
Tao Han	University of North Carolina at Charlotte, USA
Mohamad Hoseiny	University of Sydney, Australia
Wei Li	The University of Sydney, Australia
Min Luo	Services Society, USA
Rui André Oliveira	University of Lisbon, Portugal
Ju Ren	Central South University, China
Javid Taheri	Karlstad University, Sweden
Weichao Wang	University of North Carolina at Charlotte, USA
Hung-Yu Wei	National Taiwan University, Taiwan
Mengjun Xie	University of Tennessee at Chattanooga, USA
Yun Yang	Swinburne University of Technology, Australia
John Zao	Harvard University, USA

Contents

Characterization of IoT Workloads 1
   Uma Tadakamalla and Daniel A. Menascé

Latency Control for Distributed Machine Vision at the Edge
Through Approximate Computing 16
   Anjus George and Arun Ravindran

Energy-Aware Capacity Provisioning and Resource Allocation
in Edge Computing Systems 31
   Tayebeh Bahreini, Hossein Badri, and Daniel Grosu

Stackelberg Game-Theoretic Spectrum Allocation for QoE-Centric
Wireless Multimedia Communications 46
   Krishna Murthy Kattiyan Ramamoorthy, Wei Wang, and Kazem Sohraby

Intrusion Detection at the Network Edge: Solutions, Limitations,
and Future Directions 59
   Simone Raponi, Maurantonio Caprolu, and Roberto Di Pietro

Volunteer Cloud as an Edge Computing Enabler 76
   Tessema M. Mengistu, Abdullah Albuali, Abdulrahman Alahmadi,
   and Dunren Che

Author Index 85

Characterization of IoT Workloads

Uma Tadakamalla$^{(\boxtimes)}$ and Daniel A. Menascé$^{(\boxtimes)}$

Department of Computer Science, George Mason University, Fairfax, VA, USA
{utadakam,menasce}@gmu.edu

Abstract. Workload characterization is a fundamental step in carrying out performance and Quality of Service engineering studies. The workload of a system is defined as the set of all inputs received by the system from its environment during one or more time windows. The characterization of the workload entails determining the nature of its basic components as well as a quantitative and probabilistic description of the workload components in terms of both the arrival process, event counts, and service demands. Several workload characterization studies were presented for a variety of domains, except for IoT workloads. This is precisely the main contribution of this paper, which also presents a capacity planning study based on one of the workload characterizations presented here.

Keywords: Workload characterization · Internet of Things ·
Capacity planning · G/G/n queue ·
Quality of Service in edge computing

1 Introduction

Siegel et al. [35] argue that scalability is needed to support the continued expansion of the Internet of Things. Therefore, performance engineering studies are very important for understanding tradeoffs between security, availability, and response time of various types of IoT applications.

Workload characterization is a fundamental and necessary step in carrying out any performance engineering study [26]. The workload of a system is defined as the set of all inputs received by the system from its environment during one or more time windows. The characterization of the workload entails determining the nature of its basic components (e.g., transactions, I/O requests, IoT device requests) as well as a quantitative and probabilistic description of the workload components in terms of both the arrival process, event counts, and service demands (e.g., arrival rate of requests and interarrival time distributions, distribution of the number of IoT device signals received, distribution of the file sizes returned by an HTTP request) [26].

General methods for workload characterization have been discussed in [11, 12, 26]. Specific applications of these techniques to a variety of domains were developed by many researchers (see examples in Sect. 5). However, there is a need for workload characterization studies for IoT applications.

© Springer Nature Switzerland AG 2019
T. Zhang et al. (Eds.): EDGE 2019, LNCS 11520, pp. 1–15, 2019.
https://doi.org/10.1007/978-3-030-23374-7_1

The recent development of Internet of Things (IoT) and edge/fog computing demands models for this new environment. Our prior work includes the development of an analytic model, called FogQN, based on queuing networks [37] and an autonomic controller that uses FogQN to dynamically determine the optimal breakdown of processing between fog and cloud servers [38].

Any modeling effort of fog and cloud computing calls for workload characterization studies of IoT workloads. The understanding of the characteristics of IoT workloads can be used to perform capacity planning studies. These are the main contributions of this paper. More specifically, we (1) describe the methodology we used to analyze IoT traces; (2) describe and analyze three publicly available IoT datasets: NY city taxi trips, GPS trajectories of taxis in Beijing, Chicago taxi trips; and (3) present a capacity planning study based on the workload characterization of the NY city taxi trips. Our workload characterization includes counts of events, i.e., IoT device signals, at various time scales (e.g., hour of the day, day of the week) and a characterization of the interarrival time of signals received from IoT devices.

The rest of this paper is organized as follows. Section 2 describes the general data collection and analysis methodology used in this paper. Section 3 has one subsection for each of the datasets we analyzed. Each subsection describes the dataset and presents the results of the workload characterization for that dataset. Section 4 provides an example of how a queuing model can be used to answer what-if questions using the workload of NY city taxi trips. Section 5 discusses related work. Finally, Sect. 6 presents concluding remarks and future work.

2   General Data Collection and Analysis Methodology

The data collection and analysis methodology presented here can be applied to a variety of IoT workloads. This paper analyzed several publicly available IoT datasets. Some existing datasets are from applications in which data is sent by a set of sensors at regular intervals (e.g., every 5 min) in a synchronous way. We did not consider these datasets because they are not very interesting from the point of view of workload analysis. The applications we considered in our study have IoT devices that are independent of each other and send signals at irregular intervals (e.g., signals sent by a taxi cab whenever a passenger is dropped off).

Our analysis methodology consisted of the following steps:

1. Data is aggregated from all the files that make up the dataset.
2. The aggregated data is cleansed by removing any invalid and duplicate data, and any outliers.
3. The cleaned up data is sorted based on the timestamp of the records.
4. The sorted data is filtered based on characteristics such as days, hours, month, latitude/longitude of the IoT device.
5. The filtered data is characterized by computing event counts by hour of the day on a daily and monthly basis, and by day of the week.
6. The distribution of the interarrival time of signals generated by IoT devices is characterized. We used Quantile-Quantile (Q-Q) plots and Cumulative Distribution Functions (CDF) to that effect [21].

A Q-Q plot is a graphical tool that helps determine if the data points in a given data set come from the same distribution as a given theoretical distribution. A Q-Q plot is a scatter plot that plots two sets of quantiles (from the dataset and from the theoretical distribution) against each other. If both quantiles come from the same distribution, the points in the Q-Q plot form a roughly straight line. We experimented with several candidate theoretical distributions for each dataset and did a linear regression on the points. The distribution that had a coefficient of determination R^2 closest to 1 was chosen as the best fit theoretical distribution for the dataset. The candidate distributions can only be those that can take non-negative values because an interarrival time cannot be negative. For that reason we selected the lognormal, Weibull, and Gamma distributions. Note that the Weibull distribution has the exponential distribution as a special case, depending on the value of its parameters.

Table 1 presents the expressions for the probability density function (pdf) and the expressions used to compute the parameters of the three considered distributions as a function of $\bar{X}$, S and $C = S/\bar{X}$, the mean, standard deviation and coefficient of variation of the interarrival times, respectively, computed from the datasets.

Table 1. Features of the lognormal, Weibull, and Gamma distributions.

Distribution	Pdf	Parameters
Lognormal	$\frac{1}{x\sigma\sqrt{2\pi}}e^{-\frac{[\ln x - \mu]^2}{2\sigma^2}}$	$\mu = \ln(\bar{X}) - \ln(\sqrt{(1+C^2)}), \sigma = \sqrt{\ln(1+C^2)} \; \mu \in (-\infty, +\infty), \sigma \geq 0$
Weibull	$\frac{k}{\lambda}\left(\frac{x}{\lambda}\right)^{k-1}e^{-(x/\lambda)^k}$	$k \approx C^{-1.086}, \lambda = \bar{X}/\Gamma(1+1/k) \; k, \lambda > 0$
Gamma	$\frac{x^{k-1}e^{-x/\theta}}{\theta^k\Gamma(k)}$	$k = 1/C^2, \theta = S^2/\bar{X} \; k, \theta > 0$

The theoretical distribution quantile data is generated using the inverseCumulativeProbability method in the Java Apache Commons Math3 distribution package [2] with parameters computed using the equations in Table 1.

3   IoT Datasets

We describe and analyze in this section, three IoT datasets: NY city taxi trips, GPS trajectories of taxis in Beijing, and Chicago taxi trips.

3.1   New York City Taxi Trip Data

The New York City taxi trip data is provided by Illinois Data Bank, which is operated by the University of Illinois at Urbana Champaign. This dataset [15] contains records of four years (2010–2014) of taxi operations in New York City including 697,622,444 trips. The data is stored in the CSV format, organized by year and month. Each month's data is stored in a separate file. Each row in the file represents a single taxi trip. Each trip records the pickup and drop-off dates, times, and coordinates, and the metered distance reported by the taximeter. For this analysis, we only considered the drop-off date and time, drop-off latitude and longitude fields. We assumed that a fog node is at Grand Central Terminal, whose latitude and longitude coordinates are (40.7527, −73.9772), and it serves all the IoTs devices (taxis) that are within a one-mile radius. This means that signals received from the taxis at drop off locations that are within a 1-mile radius are served by the Grand Central Terminal fog node. Therefore, we selected all the records that are within 1 mile radius from the fog node for this analysis. We cleaned up the data by removing duplicate and invalid entries and used the cleaned up data to generate interarrival times. We then removed the outliers (interarrival times greater than 2000 s) from the interarrival times dataset.

Figure 1(b) shows the variation of the number of taxi signals by hour of the day for Sunday, February 7, 2010 and Monday, February 8, 2010. It is apparent that taxi cabs are utilized more on Mondays (weekday) than on Sundays (week-end), with the exception of 12:00 am through 5:00 am. This may be because more people in New York use cabs on weekdays to move around. The number of taxi signals on the early hours of Sunday exceeds the taxi cab requests during the same time on Monday because people are more likely go out on Saturday nights, and they utilize taxi cabs to get back home during the wee hours on Sunday. However, at the same time on Monday, most people are at home resting for the next work day. Also, the number of taxi signals is higher during the morning (5:00 am to 9:00 am) and evening rush hours (4:00 pm to 6:00 pm) during a Monday because between these peaks most people are more likely to be working in their offices.

Next, we analyzed the number of taxi signals for the entire month of February, 2010 grouped by hour of the day as shown in Fig. 1(a). The figure shows that the number of taxi signals is lower during non-working hours compared to those of working hours. Also, there is a clear rise in the number of signals during morning and evening rush hours from 5:00–9:00 am and 4:00–7:00 pm, respectively.

Next, we studied the variation of the number of taxi signals by days of the week and aggregated the data for each day of the week of February, 2010 as shown in Fig. 2. The figure shows that the lowest signal counts are recorded on Sundays.

We now turn our attention to the characterization of interarrival times of taxi signals using Q-Q plots and CDFs as explained in Sect. 2. To determine the best fit distribution, the quantiles of interarrival times of taxi signals were plotted against those of various theoretical distributions (i.e., lognormal, Weibull and Gamma). Table 2 shows the parameters used for each distribution and the corre-

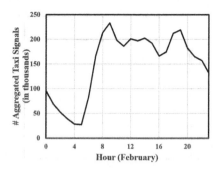 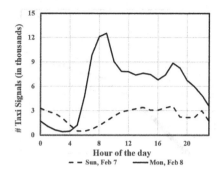

Fig. 1. (a) Left: NY Grand Central Terminal taxi signal counts aggregated by hour of the day for the entire month of February, 2010, (b) Right: NY Grand Central Terminal taxi signal counts by hour of the day for Sunday, February 7, 2010 (weekend) and Monday, February 8, 2010 (weekday)

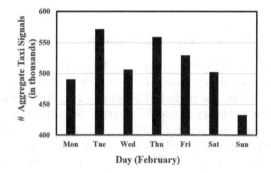

Fig. 2. NY Grand Central Terminal taxi signal counts aggregated by days of the week for February, 2010

Table 2. Fitting February 8, 2010 NY City taxi signal interarrival time data.

Distribution	Parameters	R^2
Lognormal	$\mu = -1.630$, $\sigma = 1.494$	0.941
Weibull	$k = 0.316$, $\lambda = 0.081$	0.902
Gamma	$k = 0.120$, $\theta = 4.976$	0.895

sponding R^2 value. The lognormal distribution has the best fit for the data with an R^2 value equal to 0.941. The corresponding Q-Q plot is shown in Fig. 3(a). The CDF plots of taxi signal interarrival times and the lognormal theoretical distribution are shown in Fig. 3(b). They both match very closely. Based on the R^2 value from the Q-Q plot and CDF plots, we can conclude that the data best fits the log-normal distribution.

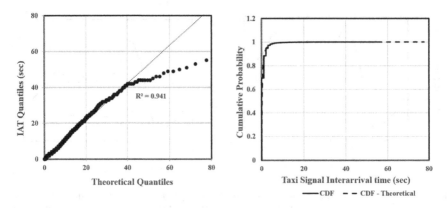

Fig. 3. (a) Q-Q plot (left) and (b) CDF plots (right) using NY Grand Central Terminal February 8, 2010 taxi signal interarrival times data and theoretical lognormal distribution data with $\mu = -1.630$ and $\sigma = 1.494$.

3.2   Microsoft T-Drive Trajectory Dataset

The Microsoft T-Drive Trajectory dataset [41] is provided by Microsoft for research purposes. This dataset contains the GPS trajectories of 10,357 taxis (one file per taxi) during the period of February 2–8, 2008 within Beijing. We ignored the data for February 2 and February 8 because they are incomplete. Each file of this dataset contains the trajectory of one taxi. The total number of points in this dataset is about 15 million and the total distance of the trajectories reaches about 9 million kilometers. We assumed that the fog node is located at Tiananmen Square, whose latitude and longitude are (39.9055, 116.3976), and that this node will serve the IoT devices (i.e., taxis) within a one-mile distance. We then selected all the records that are within a 1-mile radius from that node and used that data to generate the interarrival times of the signals. We then removed the outliers from the interarrival times data.

Figure 4(b) shows the the variation of the number of taxi signals by hour of the day for Sunday, February 3, 2008, and Monday, February 4, 2008. It is apparent that taxi cabs are utilized less over the night hours than during day time. Also, there are more taxis utilized during evening hours on weekends than weekdays.

Next, we analyzed the number of taxi signals from February 3–7, 2008 grouped by hour of the day as shown in Fig. 4(a). The figure shows that the number of taxi signals is lower during night hours than during day time. A similar trend was seen in Fig. 5. This figure shows the variation of the number of taxi signals by days of the week from February 3–7, 2008. The highest number of taxi signals on weekdays can be seen on Mondays and it decreases through the week. The second highest number is observed on Sundays maybe because Tiananmen Square is a popular place for visitors and there are more visitors on weekends than on weekdays.

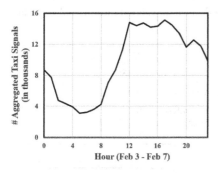 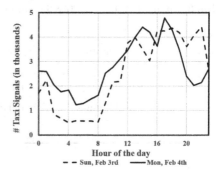

Fig. 4. (a) Left: Beijing Tiananmen Square taxi signal counts aggregated by hour of the day for February 3–7, 2008, (b) Right: Beijing Tiananmen Square taxi signal counts by hour of the day for Sunday, February 3, 2008 (weekend day) and Monday, February 4, 2008 (weekday).

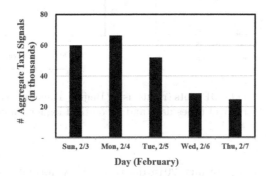

Fig. 5. Beijing's Tiananmen Square taxi signal counts aggregated by days of the week.

Next, we characterized the interarrival times of taxi signals using Q-Q plots and CDFs as explained in Sect. 2. To determine the best fit distribution, the quantiles of interarrival times of taxi signals were plotted against those of various theoretical distributions (i.e., lognormal, Weibull and Gamma). Table 3 shows the parameters used for each distribution and the corresponding R^2 value.

The lognormal distribution has the best fit for the data with an R^2 value equal to 0.986. The corresponding Q-Q plot is shown in Fig. 6(a). The CDF plot of taxi signal interarrival times and lognormal theoretical distribution is shown in Fig. 6(b). They both match very closely. Based on the R^2 value from the Q-Q plot and CDF plots, we can conclude that the data best fits a lognormal distribution.

3.3 Chicago Taxi Trips Dataset

The Chicago taxi trips dataset provided by the City of Chicago's open data portal [1] contains information on taxi trips in Chicago reported to the City of

Table 3. Fitting February 5, 2008 Tiananmen Square taxi signal interarrival time data.

Distribution	Parameters	R^2
Lognormal	$\mu = -0.130$, $\sigma = 1.111$	0.986
Weibull	$k = 0.616$, $\lambda = 1.119$	0.974
Gamma	$k = 0.410$, $\theta = 3.970$	0.946

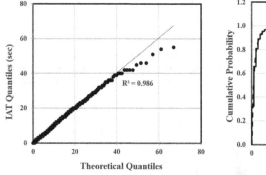 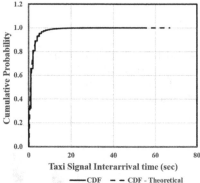

Fig. 6. Q-Q plot (left) and CDF plots (right) using Beijing Tiananmen Square February 5, 2008 taxi signal interarrival times data and theoretical lognormal distribution data with $\mu = -0.130$ and $\sigma = 1.111$.

Chicago. We exported February 2015 data in a CSV format using their API. Each record in the file represents a single taxi trip and includes pickup and drop-off dates, times, and coordinates, and trip duration (in sec). The pickup and drop-off times are rounded to the nearest 15 min and the trip duration is rounded to the nearest minute, meaning that the trip durations are in multiples of 60 s. For this analysis, we only considered the trip end time (trip start time + trip duration), drop off latitude and longitude fields. We assumed that the fog node is at Millennium Park, whose latitude and longitude are (41.8826, −87.6226), and it serves all the IoT devices (taxis) that are within one-mile radius. Therefore, we selected all taxi trip records whose drop off location is within one-mile radius from the fog node for this analysis. We cleaned up the data by removing records with missing data and used the clean data for taxi trip count analysis. To compute the interarrival times, we grouped the taxi signals reported each minute and computed the interarrival times by distributing them uniformly within that minute.

Figure 7(b) shows the variation of the number of taxi signals by hour of the day for Sunday, February 22, 2015 and Monday, February 23, 2015. It is apparent that taxi cabs are utilized more on Mondays (weekday) than on Sundays (weekend), with the exception of 12:00 am through 6:00 am. This may be because more people in Chicago use taxis on weekdays to move around than on weekends. The number of taxi signals on the early hours of Sunday exceeds the taxi signals during the same time on Monday because more people are likely to go out on Saturday nights than on Sunday nights, and they utilize taxis to get back home in the early hours of the next day. Also, the number of taxi signals is higher during the morning (6:00 am to 9:00 am) and evening rush hours (3:00 pm to 6:00 pm) during a Monday (weekday) because people are more likely to use taxis to go to work and go back home during these times.

Next, we analyzed the number of taxi signals for the entire month of February, 2015 grouped by hour of the day as shown in Fig. 7(a). The figure shows that the number of taxi signals is lower during non-working hours compared to those of working hours. Also, there is a clear rise in the number of signals during morning and evening rush hours from 5:00 am to 9:00 am and 3:00 pm to 6:00 pm, respectively.

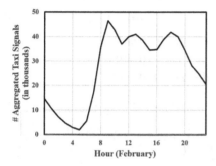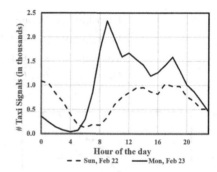

Fig. 7. Chicago Millennium Park taxi signal counts. (a) Left: aggregated by hour of the day for the entire month of February 2015, (b) Right: by hour of the day for Sunday, February 22, 2015 (weekend) and Monday, February 23, 2015 (weekday).

Next, we studied the variation of the number of taxi signals by days of the month and aggregated the data for each day of the month of February as shown in Fig. 8(a). The figure shows that the signal counts are higher on weekdays than on weekends and the lowest signal counts are seen on Sundays every week.

Next, we studied the variation of the number of taxi signals by day of the week and aggregated the data for each day of the week of February 2015 as shown in Fig. 8(b). The figure shows that the weekday counts are higher than the weekend counts and increase from Monday to Friday. Also, lowest signal counts are recorded on Sundays.

We then characterized the interarrival times of taxi signals using Q-Q plots and CDFs as explained in Sect. 2. To determine the best fit distribution, the quantiles of interarrival times of taxi signals were plotted against those of various theoretical distributions (i.e., lognormal, Weibull and Gamma). Table 4 shows the parameters used for each distribution and the corresponding R^2 value.

The R^2 for lognormal and Weibull distributions are very close. However, the lognormal distribution has the best fit for the data with an R^2 value equal to

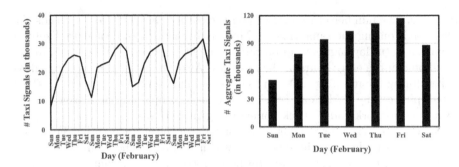

Fig. 8. Chicago Millennium Park taxi signal counts. (a) Left: for each day in February 2015 (b) Right: aggregated by days of the week in February 2015.

Table 4. Fitting February 23, 2015 Chicago taxi signal interarrival time data

Distribution	Parameters	R^2
Lognormal	$\mu = 0.241,\ \sigma = 1.439$	0.9621
Weibull	$k = 0.35,\ \lambda = 0.71$	0.9618
Gamma	$k = 0.144,\ \theta = 24.809$	0.7977

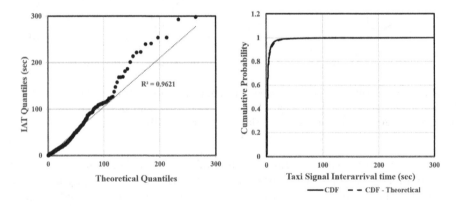

Fig. 9. Q-Q plot (left) and CDF plots (right) using the Chicago Millennium Park February 23, 2015 taxi signal interarrival times and theoretical lognormal distribution data with $\mu = 0.241$ and $\sigma = 1.439$.

0.9621. The corresponding Q-Q plot is shown in Fig. 9(a) and the plots for the CDF of interarrival times and the lognormal theoretical distribution are shown in Fig. 9(b). They both match very closely. Based on the R^2 value from the Q-Q plot and CDF plots, we can conclude that the data best fits a lognormal distribution even though a Weibull distribution would be a good fit also.

4   Workload Characterization Use in Capacity Planning

As indicated above, workload characterization is an essential step for capacity planning purposes. Consider the following what-if question: How many fog servers are required to support a given load with an average response time below a certain value? We show here how we can answer this type of question using the NY City taxi workload. Let n be the number of fog servers that handle signals received from taxis within a one-mile radius of a given location. All arriving signals join a single queue and are dispatched to the first available fog server when they reach the head of the line.

The average response time of a taxi signal was computed using the approximate G/G/n queuing equation given below [26]

$$T \approx E[S] + \frac{C(\rho, n)}{c(1 - \rho)/E[S]} \times \frac{C_a^2 + C_s^2}{2} \tag{1}$$

where $E[S]$ is the average processing time of a taxi signal, $\rho = \lambda E[S]/n$ is the utilization of the set of n fog servers that receive a collective average arrival rate of λ taxi signals/sec, C_a is the coefficient of variation (i.e., the ratio of the standard deviation by the mean) of the interarrival time, C_s is the coefficient of variation of the service time, and $C(\rho, n)$ is the Erlang formula given by

$$C(\rho, n) = \frac{(n\rho)^n/n!}{(1 - \rho) \sum_{j=0}^{n-1} (n\rho)^j/j! + (n\rho)^n/n!}. \tag{2}$$

Because the utilization ρ must be less than 1, we have that $\lambda < n/E[S]$, i.e., the average arrival rate cannot exceed $n/E[S]$. Our data showed that the maximum rate of signals received from taxis within a one-mile radius from Grand Central Terminal during the date of February 8, 2010 was approximately 4 signals/sec. We used the G/G/n equations above to compute the variation of the average signal response time as a function of the average arrival rate λ for five values of n (see Fig. 10). We used the following numerical values for Fig. 10: $E[S] = 0.2\,\text{s}$, $C_a = 2.88$, $C_s = 0.94$ (from 2/8/2010 data). As expected, the figure shows that the maximum arrival rate of signals that can be handled increases in proportion to the number of fog servers. For example, when $n = 1$, the maximum arrival rate the system can handle has to be less than 5 signals/sec whereas for $n = 5$, the maximum arrival rate the system can handle has to be less than 25 signals/sec. Additionally, the average response time decreases as n increases for a given arrival rate. For example, at an arrival rate $= 4.5$ signals/sec the average response time with one server is 9.13 s whereas with 5 servers the average response time is 0.2 s. If we want the average response time not to exceed 1 s for an average arrival rate of taxi signals of 10 signals/sec we need at least 3 fog servers.

5   Related Work

Workload characterization studies have been conducted for various types of applications and systems. Some examples include: e-commerce [25], auction

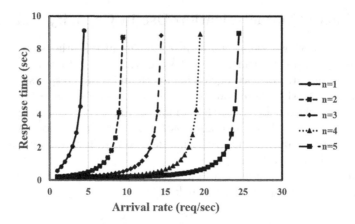

Fig. 10. Average response time vs. arrival rate for $n = 1, 2, 3, 4, 5$

sites [5], WWW [24], networking [28,30], live streaming media [39], spam traffic [19], storage systems [36], data centers [32], cloud computing [23], grid computing [14], memory systems [8], and database systems [16]. [27] quantifies a Poisson process approximation for IoT aggregate arrival processes. The studies above have shown that different domains have their own specific workload characteristics. Our paper fills a much needed gap in terms of understanding and characterizing IoT workloads.

The vision and challenges of edge computing were discussed in [9,34]. There are some very good IoT and fog/edge computing surveys: a survey of mobile edge computing was presented in [3]; a survey of architecture, enabling technologies, security and privacy, and IoT applications was presented in [22]; and Ngu et al. presented a survey on IoT middleware [29]. Cruz et al. presented a reference model for IoT middleware [13]. [33] presents an IoT architecture based on transparent computing to build scalable IoT platforms. Transparent computing enables users to select services on-demand, without being concerned with the installation and management of services.

Similarly to [38], the work in [40] aims at reducing the response time of IoT applications by offloading the load of fog-capable devices to the cloud. Another work along the same vein is [10]. Fan and Ansari [17] presented an application aware scheme to allocate IoT-based workloads to edge servers in order to minimize the response time of IoT applications. The work in [4] proposes a method for reducing latency and device energy consumption using the fog, which is based on computational offloading and network utility optimization. The work in [18] presents a vision of human-centered edge-device based computing, known as Edge-centric Computing and the research challenges associated with its implementation. The work in [7] proposed a new technique called Home Edge Computing, a three-tier edge computing architecture that provides data storage and processing near the users (home server) to achieve ultra-low latency.

The work in [20] analyzed a motion dataset to characterize the kinetic energy that can be harvested by an IoT node and developed energy allocation algorithms for such nodes. The work by Pereira et al. [31] discusses an experimental evaluation of latency in IoT service composition with mobile gateways and assesses the capabilities and limitations of a standard machine-to-machine middleware. IoT devices with security flaws are attractive targets for attacks. [6] discusses HoneyScope, a network centric approach to protect vulnerable IoT devices by creating virtualized views of the network and nodes.

None of the studies cited above present a comprehensive workload characterization of actual IoT applications.

6   Concluding Remarks and Future Work

Understanding and quantitatively characterizing the workload generated by IoT devices is key to being able to analyze the performance of edge/fog computing environments. Our study analyzed three datasets that contain information generated by taxis in three big cities. Our workload characterization, which can be applied to other IoT workloads, included counts of events, i.e., IoT device signals, at various time scales (e.g., hour of the day, day of the week) and a characterization of the interarrival time of signals received from IoT devices.

Our results indicated that the interarrival time of IoT signals for all three datasets can be very well approximated by a lognormal distribution. We also observed that the count of events for the three taxi-related datasets can be well explained by expected daily routines of habitants of large cities. We also showed that workload characterization results can be used for capacity planning studies of edge computing environments.

In the future, we intend to apply our characterization methodology to IoT datasets that deal with other types of IoT devices. We are also investigating the sensitivity of our results with respect to the location of the fog node, and how it may affect the probability distribution and parameters of the request interarrival times.

References

1. Chicago data portal. https://data.cityofchicago.org/
2. Package org.apache.commons.math3.distribution. http://commons.apache. org/proper/commons-math/javadocs/api-3.5/org/apache/commons/math3/ distribution/package-summary.html
3. Abbas, N., Zhang, Y., Taherkordi, A., Skeie, T.: Mobile edge computing: a survey. IEEE Internet Things J. 5(1), 450–465 (2018)
4. Ahn, S., Gorlatova, M., Chiang, M.: Leveraging fog and cloud computing for efficient computational offloading. In: 2017 Undergraduate Research Technology Conference (URTC), IEEE MIT, pp. 1–4. IEEE (2017)
5. Akula, V., Menasce, D.: Two-level workload characterization of online auctions. Electron. Commer. Res. Appl. 6, 192–208 (2007)
6. Al-Shaer, E., Wei, J., Hamlen, K.W., Wang, C.: HONEYSCOPE: IoT device protection with deceptive network views. Autonomous Cyber Deception, pp. 167–181. Springer, Cham (2019). https://doi.org/10.1007/978-3-030-02110-8_9

7. Babou, C.S.M., Fall, D., Kashihara, S., Niang, I., Kadobayashi, Y.: Home edge computing (HEC): design of a new edge computing technology for achieving ultra-low latency. In: Liu, S., Tekinerdogan, B., Aoyama, M., Zhang, L.-J. (eds.) EDGE 2018. LNCS, vol. 10973, pp. 3–17. Springer, Cham (2018). https://doi.org/10.1007/978-3-319-94340-4_1

8. Barroso, L.A., Gharachorloo, K., Bugnion, E.: Memory system characterization of commercial workloads. In: Proceedings of 25th Annual International Symposium Computer Architecture, ISCA 1998, pp. 3–14. IEEE Computer Society, Washington, DC (1998)

9. Bonomi, F., Milito, R., Zhu, J., Addepalli, S.: Fog computing and its role in the Internet of Things. In: Proceedings of MCC Workshop on Mobile Cloud Computing, MCC 2012, pp. 13–16, New York, NY, USA. ACM (2012)

10. Brogi, A., Forti, S.: QoS-aware deployment of IoT applications through the fog. IEEE Internet Things J. **4**(5), 1185–1192 (2017)

11. Calzarossa, M., Massari, L., Tessera, D.: Workload characterization issues and methodologies. In: Haring, G., Lindemann, C., Reiser, M. (eds.) Performance Evaluation: Origins and Directions. LNCS, vol. 1769, pp. 459–482. Springer, Heidelberg (2000). https://doi.org/10.1007/3-540-46506-5_20

12. Calzarossa, M., Serazzi, G.: Workload characterization. Proc. IEEE **81**, 1136–1150 (1993)

13. da Cruz, M.A.A., Rodrigues, J.J.P.C., Al-Muhtadi, J., Korotaev, V.V., de Albuquerque, V.H.C.: A reference model for Internet of Things middleware. IEEE Internet Things J. **5**(2), 871–883 (2018)

14. Di, S., Kondo, D., Cirne, W.: Characterization and comparison of cloud versus grid workloads. In: 2012 IEEE International Conference Cluster Computing, pp. 230–238, September 2012

15. Donovan, D., Work, D.B.: New york city taxi trip data (2010–2013) (2016)

16. Elnaffar, S., Martin, P., Horman, R.: Automatically classifying database workloads. In: Proceedings of 11th International Conference Information and Knowledge Management, CIKM 2002, pp. 622–624, New York, NY, USA. ACM (2002)

17. Fan, Q., Ansari, N.: Application aware workload allocation for edge computing-based IoT. IEEE Internet Things J. **5**(3), 2146–2153 (2018)

18. Garcia Lopez, P., et al.: Edge-centric computing: vision and challenges. SIGCOMM Comput. Commun. Rev. **45**(5), 37–42 (2015)

19. Gomes, L.H., Cazita, C., Almeida, J.M., Almeida, V., Meira, Jr., W.: Characterizing a spam traffic. In: Proceedings of 4th ACM SIGCOMM Conference Internet Measurement, IMC 2004, pp. 356–369, New York, NY, USA. ACM (2004)

20. Gorlatova, M., Sarik, J., Grebla, G., Cong, M., Kymissis, I., Zussman, G.: Movers and shakers: kinetic energy harvesting for the Internet of Things. In: The 2014 ACM International Conference on Measurement and Modeling of Computer Systems, SIGMETRICS 2014, pp. 407–419, New York, NY, USA. ACM (2014)

21. Jain, R.: The Art of Computer Systems Performance Analysis. Wiley, Hoboken (1991)

22. Lin, J., Yu, W., Zhang, N., Yang, X., Zhang, H., Zhao, W.: A survey on Internet of Things: architecture, enabling technologies, security and privacy, and applications. IEEE Internet Things J. **4**(5), 1125–1142 (2017)

23. Magalhaes, D., Calheiros, R.N., Buyya, R., Gomes, D.G.: Workload modeling for resource usage analysis and simulation in cloud computing. Comput. Electr. Eng. **47**, 69–81 (2015)

24. Menascé, D., Abrahao, B., Barbará, D., Almeida, V., Ribeiro, F.: Fractal characterization of web workloads. In: Eleventh International World Wide Web Conference, Honolulu, HI, pp. 7–11 (2002)
25. Menasce, D., Almeida, V., Fonseca, R., Mendes, M.: A methodology for workload characterization of e-commerce sites. In: Proceedings of 1st ACM Conference on Electronic Commerce, EC 1999, pp. 119–128, New York, NY, USA. ACM (1999)
26. Menasce, D.A., Almeida, V.A.F., Dowdy, L.W.: Performance by Design: Computer Capacity Planning by Example. Prentice Hall, Upper Saddle River (2004)
27. Metzger, F., Hofeld, T., Bauer, A., Kounev, S., Heegaard, P.E.: Modeling of aggregated IoT traffic and its application to an IoT cloud. Proc. IEEE **107**(4), 679–694 (2019)
28. Nedyalkov, I., Stefanov, A., Georgiev, G.: Characterization of the traffic in IP-based communication networks. In: 2018 International Conference on High Technology for Sustainable Development (HiTech), pp. 1–4. IEEE (2018)
29. Ngu, A.H., Gutierrez, M., Metsis, V., Nepal, S., Sheng, Q.Z.: IoT middleware: a survey on issues and enabling technologies. IEEE Internet Things J. **4**(1), 1–20 (2017)
30. Paxson, V., Floyd, S.: Wide area traffic: the failure of poisson modeling. IEEE/ACM Trans. Netw. **3**(3), 226–244 (1995)
31. Pereira, C., Pinto, A., Ferreira, D., Aguiar, A.: Experimental characterization of mobile IoT application latency. IEEE Internet Things J. **4**(4), 1082–1094 (2017)
32. Postema, B.F., Geuze, N.J., Haverkort, B.R.: Fitting realistic data centre workloads: a data science approach. In: Proceedings of the Ninth International Conference on Future Energy Systems, e-Energy 2018, pp. 486–491, New York, NY, USA. ACM (2018)
33. Ren, J., Guo, H., Xu, C., Zhang, Y.: Serving at the edge: a scalable IoT architecture based on transparent computing. IEEE Netw. **31**(5), 96–105 (2017)
34. Shi, W., Cao, J., Zhang, Q., Li, Y., Xu, L.: Edge computing: vision and challenges. IEEE Internet Things J. **3**(5), 637–646 (2016)
35. Siegel, J.E., Kumar, S., Sarma, S.E.: The future Internet of Things: secure, efficient, and model-based. IEEE Internet Things J. **5**(4), 2386–2398 (2018)
36. Smirni, E., Reed, D.: Lessons from characterizing the input/output behavior of parallel scientific applications. Perform. Eval. **33**(1), 27–44 (1998)
37. Tadakamalla, U., Menasce, D.A.: FogQN: an analytic model for fog/cloud computing. In: Proceedings of 1st Workshop on Managed Fog-to-Cloud (mF2C), joint with 11th IEEE/ACM International Conference on Utility and Cloud Computing. IEEE/ACM (2018). https://www.cs.gmu.edu/~menasce/papers/mF2C2018TM.pdf
38. Tadakamalla, U., Menasce, D.A.: Autonomic resource management using analytic models for fog/cloud computing. In: Proceedings of IEEE International Conference on Fog Computing. IEEE (2019)
39. Veloso, E., Almeida, V., Meira, W., Bestavros, A., Jin, S.: A hierarchical characterization of a live streaming media workload. In: Proceedings of 2nd ACM SIGCOMM Workshop on Internet Measurement, IMW 2002, pp. 117–130, New York, NY, USA. ACM (2002)
40. Yousefpour, A., Ishigaki, G., Gour, R., Jue, J.P.: On reducing IoT service delay via fog offloading. IEEE Internet Things J. **5**(2), 998–1010 (2018)
41. Zheng, Y.: T-drive trajectory data sample, August 2011. https://www.microsoft.com/en-us/research/publication/t-drive-trajectory-data-sample/

Latency Control for Distributed Machine Vision at the Edge Through Approximate Computing

Anjus George$^{(\boxtimes)}$ and Arun Ravindran

University of North Carolina at Charlotte, Charlotte, NC, USA
`ageorg28@uncc.edu`

Abstract. Multicamera based Deep Learning vision applications subscribe to the Edge computing paradigm due to stringent latency requirements. However, guaranteeing latency in the wireless communication links between the cameras nodes and the Edge server is challenging, especially in the cheap and easily available unlicensed bands due to the interference from other camera nodes in the system, and from external sources. In this paper, we show how approximate computation techniques can be used to design a latency controller that uses multiple video frame image quality control knobs to simultaneously satisfy latency and accuracy requirements for machine vision applications involving object detection, and human pose estimation. Our experimental results on an Edge test bed indicate that the controller is able to correct for up to 164% degradation in latency due to interference within a settling time of under 1.15 s.

Keywords: Edge computing · Machine vision ·
Approximate computing · Latency control

1 Introduction

The recent emergence of powerful Deep Learning algorithms, along with the capacity to store and process massive amounts of data, has given us the ability to potentially recognize objects in near real-time [13]. Such real-time machine vision is a foundational technology in a number of applications such as automatic video surveillance, augmented and virtual reality, autonomous driving, and robotics. In many of these applications, timely recognition of objects and their activity is important since events need to be responded within tight deadline constraints precluding the offloading of computation to the Cloud. The latency critical nature of machine vision applications motivates the use of the Edge computing paradigm [5,6,14,23,24] where compute and storage are done at the Edge of the network close to the camera.

As a concrete motivating example, in a surveillance application (for example, to detect/predict pedestrian accidents), the Edge vision system consists of

© Springer Nature Switzerland AG 2019
T. Zhang et al. (Eds.): EDGE 2019, LNCS 11520, pp. 16–30, 2019.
https://doi.org/10.1007/978-3-030-23374-7_2

multiple video cameras monitoring an area of interest (for example, a traffic intersection) from different vantage points. In dense urban environments, where occlusions are common, multiple camera views increase tracking robustness. The cameras transmit the video frames to an Edge server located in the vicinity. The Edge server aggregates video frames from multiple cameras, and executes Deep Learning based machine vision algorithms to determine/predict events of interest (for example, potential pedestrian accidents). Due to cost and ease of installation reasons, the communication link between the camera and the Edge server is wireless, operating in the unlicensed bands (for example, WiFi). Events such as predicting of pedestrian accidents, are latency critical, necessitating careful design of the compute and communication at the Edge to ensure that latency bounds specified by the application are met. While hardware accelerators (for example, GPUs, FPGAs) can be used to minimize compute latency, the wireless links between the camera and Edge nodes are prone to large variations in the latency due to interference, both from peer camera nodes, and unrelated external sources.

In this paper, we describe the use of approximate computing to meet latency requirements at the Edge in the presence of large latency variations in the wireless communication link. Approximate computing is based on the idea that in some applications, selective inaccuracies in computation can be tolerated to achieve gains in efficiency [17]. Machine vision applications can potentially tolerate approximate computing since selective loss of image quality may still not impact object/event detection accuracy adversely. We use this observation to design a controller that dynamically uses multiple video image frame quality control knobs to simultaneously maintain application specified latency, and object/pose detection accuracy in the presence of interference in the wireless communication channel.

The paper makes the following contributions -

- Investigates the applicability of approximate computing by characterizing the impact of image quality on application accuracy for Deep Learning based vision applications.
- Identifies multiple control knobs for controlling image quality, and characterizes their impact on wireless channel latency.
- Presents the design of a latency controller that uses the approximate computing paradigm to simultaneously achieve application specified latency and accuracy in the presence of unpredictable channel interference.
- Experimentally demonstrates the operation of the controller on an Edge test bed for two machine vision applications involving object detection, and human pose estimation.

To the best of our knowledge, this is the first work that uses approximate computing to control communication latency at the Edge for machine vision applications.

The rest of the paper is organized as follows - Sect. 2, gives a brief overview of related work on machine vision at the Edge, and the different applications of approximate computing. Section 3 provides a system level description of distributed machine vision at the Edge. Section 4 describes the Edge test bed and presents the experimental characterization of wireless channel latency. Section 5 then presents our study of the impact of image quality on application accuracy for Deep Learning based machine vision applications. Section 6, presents the design of the controller, followed by experimental evaluation and results in Sect. 7. Section 8 concludes the paper with summary of our work, with suggestions for future research directions.

2   Related Work

The concept and motivation behind Edge computing have been described in a number of recent publications [5,6,9,14,21–25]. Regarding machine vision at the Edge, in the Gabriel project [10], Ha et. al. describe a wearable cognitive assistance system where the images captured by a mobile device are processed by the Edge node to analyze what the user is seeing, and provide the user with cues as to what is in the scene (for example, recognizing a person). In the VisFlow project, Lu et al. [16] describe a system that can analyze feeds from multiple cameras for license plate recognition and real-time traffic flow mapping. However, in contrast to our work, none of these works address guaranteeing of latency requirements at the Edge for machine vision applications. In the Hetero-Edge project, Zhang et. al. [26] describe a system that can efficiently orchestrate real-time vision applications on heterogeneous Edge servers. The new resource orchestration platform developed, uses a set of task scheduling schemes to make the Hetero-Edge system latency-aware, but does not consider communication latency.

In [17], Mittal provides a survey of approximate computing techniques. Strategies for approximation at the code level such as loop perforation, and at the architecture level such as reduced precision operations are discussed. Regarding applications of approximate computing to Deep Learning, Chen et al. [8] use approximate computing to accelerate network training, while Ibrahim et. al. [12] explore the use of approximate computing to realize Deep Learning networks on resource constrained embedded platforms. Unlike our work, in these works approximate computing is targeted towards reducing the computational load. In [4], Betzel et. al. introduce the concept of approximate communication to reduce the communication between processing elements in a high performance computing system. They evaluate compression, reduced synchronization, and value prediction as potential approximate communication techniques. While we use approximate communication as well, in contrast to Betzel et. al. we target latency variations due to interference in wireless communication channels, and investigate the impact of the approximation communication on computing, by evaluating its impact on the application accuracy.

In [18], Pakha et. al. introduce the idea of control knobs to parametrize a custom video protocol that streams videos from cameras to cloud servers to perform neural-network-based video analytics. The new server driven protocol highlights opportunities to improve the tradeoffs between bandwidth usage and inference accuracy, but does not address Edge specific latency requirements demanded by Deep Learning vision applications.

3   System Architecture

The overarching motivation behind the design of our system is to make available real-time video frames from multiple cameras to Deep Learning surveillance applications at the Edge for analytics, detection and prediction of a diverse set of events/objects while being scalable. A subset of such applications include, pedestrian safety guidance, road accident prediction, drunken driver detection and crime detection in public spaces. As shown in Fig. 1 the physical model of our system consists of multiple embedded boards equipped with video cameras communicating to an Edge server through WiFi (802.11ac) wireless routers. The cameras monitor video scenes from different angles in a particular area of interest (e.g., traffic intersection, parking lot). The camera nodes are deployed in the field (for example, at the traffic intersection poles), whereas the Edge node (Edge server) is assumed to be in a more

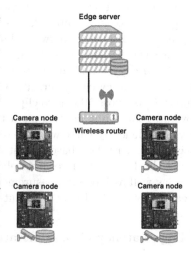

Fig. 1. Distributed machine vision at the Edge. Multiple camera nodes transmit video frames to an Edge server through a wireless communication link. The Edge server runs Deep Learning based machine vision algorithm for object/event detection and prediction.

secure place (for example, traffic signal box). The camera nodes are assumed to have limited compute and storage resources compared to the Edge nodes.

4   Characterizing Wireless Latency at the Edge

In this section we describe the test bed to characterize wireless latency at the Edge. In particular, we are interested in determining latency variations seen at the Edge due to interference, as well as potential means to control it.

4.1   Edge Test Bed

Our Edge test bed consists of two video camera equipped NVIDIA Jetson TX2 boards with 256 CUDA core Pascal GPU and quadcore ARM Cortex-A57 processor. A laptop with Intel Core i7 processor and Nvidia GeForce 1060 GPU serves as the Edge server. The Jetson boards and the laptop run Linux. The wireless link consists of a NETGEAR Nighthawk XR700 access point that uses 802.11ac (5 GHz) standard with a bandwidth of up to 7.2 Gbps. The Edge server is connected to the access point through Ethernet, while the Jetson TX2 boards connect to the access point through the 802.11ac WiFi link.

The initial workload consisted of several pedestrian car accident surveillance videos from YouTube. These videos are obtained from real-life incidents where the pedestrian is struck by an automobile. In order to demonstrate the reproducibility of image size tuning knobs and accuracy characterization for Egde vision benchmarks, we used two publicly available workloads, namely, CADP [19] and JAAD [20] data sets. Both data sets consist of videos captured under various camera types and qualities in different weather/lighting conditions. To perform the accuracy characterization for object detection and pose estimation benchmarks, we chose 100 video clips each from the CADP and JAAD data sets. The overall goal of our multi-camera Edge vision system in this case would be to provide sufficiently early warning to pedestrians and drivers to avoid potential accidents. A Python based client and multi-threaded server at the camera node and the Edge server respectively, facilitate camera node to server image transfer, as well as latency measurements. The wireless latency and bandwidth are measured with the Linux Qperf utility.

4.2   Edge Latency Characterization

We initially characterized the image transfer latency from camera node to the Edge server, for different image sizes, with the camera node at different distances from the access point. This setup emulates an Edge operational scenario where image sizes vary depending on the scene content, and the cameras node may be placed at different distances from the wireless access point so as to get the best visual coverage of the scene. Figure 2a shows the variation in latency (plotted on the y-axis), at different image sizes (plotted on the x-axis). Figure 2b plots the latency measurements taken at differing camera node distance. In both cases, each measurement point is an average of 10 measurements. We note that the latency approximately increases linearly with size. This results suggests that for camera nodes at fixed locations, the latency can be tuned by varying the size of the image.

To study the impact of interference when two camera nodes are transmitting simultaneously, we set up the camera node under test at a distance of 5 m away from the access point, and the second camera node at a distance of 3 m. Both camera nodes continuously transmit image frames to the Edge server. Figure 3 shows that the interference causes the test camera node to suffer a latency increase as high as 164 %.

As seen from this experiment, the latency for image frame transfer from camera node to Edge server varies dramatically in an unpredictable communication environment at the Edge. Since many camera nodes might be operating in a given Edge vision system, counter measures have to be taken to mitigate this increase in latency due to interference for latency critical Edge vision applications.

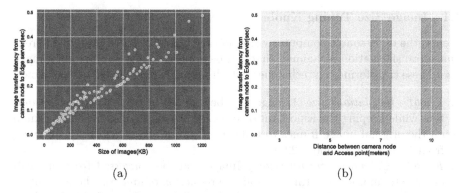

(a)   (b)

Fig. 2. (a) Image transfer latency from camera node to the Edge server vs. image size with distance between camera node and wireless access point fixed to 10 m (b) Image transfer latency from camera node to the Edge server vs. distance between camera node and wireless access point for an image size of 1.2 MB

5   Approximate Computing for Latency Control

Approximate computing (AC) exploits the gap between the extent of accuracy needed by the applications and that provided by the computing system, for achieving various optimizations [17]. AC leverages the fact that a number of vital applications, like machine learning and multimedia processing, do not essentially have to yield accurate results to be useful [3]. In these applications, we can drop some images or lower the image resolution, provided that, the deep vision applications' accuracy does not suffer substantially.

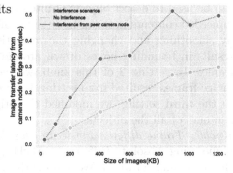

Fig. 3. Image transfer latency from camera node to the Edge server vs. image size in presence of interference from peer camera node

As seen in our experimental evaluation of latency in Sect. 4, channel interference from other camera nodes can cause channel latency to increase. We also note that for fixed camera node locations, tuning the image size is a potential means to control latency. However, reducing the information content in the images could make them unusable for object/event detection/prediction vision applications. In this section we explore potential modifications that can be done on images through which we can modify the image content and thus vary the image sizes. We call these modifications as tuning knobs for images. We present five such tuning knobs - resolution, color space modifications, blurring, choice of detection techniques, and choice of frame differencing techniques. We then study the impact of these tuning knobs on accuracy of two machine vision benchmarks.

5.1 Image Size Tuning Knobs

We use the open source computer vision library OpenCV [2] to explore different image transformation techniques that can be applied to images to modify image size. These transformation techniques (which we call tuning knobs) are as follows:

1. *Knob1 - Resolution:* Size of images can be reduced by decreasing their resolution while keeping the aspect ratio constant. We applied the resolution knob on the original image frames to tune them into different resolutions varying from 1280×720 to 400×225.
2. *Knob2 - Colorspace modifications:* Images can be converted from one colorspace to another resulting in total size reduction of images. There are more than 150 color-space conversion methods available in OpenCV [2]. We chose BGR↔Gray, BGR↔HSV, BGR↔LAB and BGR↔LUV colorspace modifications.
3. *Knob3 - Blurring:* Image frames can be blurred by passing them through various low pass filters. The cv2.blur() [2] method from OpenCV blurs an image using normalized box filter. We tuned this knob by inserting blurring filter kernel sizes of (5,5), (8,8), (10,10) and (15,15).
4. *Knob4 - Image detection techniques:* Different image detection techniques can be used to detect objects of interest in the image frames and remove the unneeded contents in them. In setting 1 of this knob, we pre-processed images by smoothing and changing the resolution to detect moving objects. This results in bounding boxes drawn around the detected objects in the image frames. In setting 2 of this knob, we modified the bounding box detected image frames resulted from setting 1, by removing all the stationary objects. In the third setting, we modified the original images by retaining only the contours of all the objects.
5. *Knob5 - Frame differencing techniques:* We applied frame differencing technique using Absolute Difference (AbsDiff) [2] to identify the keyframes from the set of image frames. We assume that, more the dissimilarity between the image frames, more the useful information that can be extracted from those images. Hence it is acceptable to drop similar images within a threshold. We chose the threshold values in such a way that 11.6%, 22.3%, 30.3% and 40.1% of the frames are dropped from a total set of image frames.

5.2 Machine Vision Benchmarks

To study the impact of object detection accuracy on the image frames after modifying them using different tuning knob combinations, we selected two machine vision applications - object detection and human pose estimation. These applications, executing on the Edge server, serve as benchmarks to evaluate the worthiness of the images modified using the tuning knobs. The input videos are drawn from the pedestrian accident videos described in Sect. 4.1.

1. *Object detection using MobileNet-SSD:* One of the popular object detection Deep Learning algorithm suited to resource constrained devices is Single Shot

Detectors (SSDs) [15]. We used pre-trained MobileNet model, specifically designed for embedded vision applications, trained using Caffe-SSD framework [1,11]. The model detects objects such as cars, persons and plants in the original image frames as well as in the modified image frames (all knob combinations). We calculate the True Positive Rate (TPR) for each setting for all the knobs (including the unmodified frames) based on the manually verified ground truth. TPR measures the actual positives that are identified as such. Figure 4a visually shows the impact of applying tuning knobs 2 and 3 to a video frame from the pedestrian accident videos described in Sect. 4.1.

2. *Pose estimation using OpenPose:* Pose estimation deals with localizing human body parts for applications such as augmented reality, animation, fitness and health. The OpenPose project from CMU [7] is an open source real-time multi person system to detect human body, hand and facial keypoints ((x,y) coordinates of different body parts) on single images. The input to OpenPose can be images or videos from webcam, Flir/Point Grey or IP camera. When given these inputs, the software outputs the video frames and keypoints in different formats. We input the original and modified image frames to Open-Pose to generate the pose detected image frames and keypoint locations. We enabled single person tracking feature in OpenPose to obtain keypoints and their confidence levels for a single pedestrian in our images. We also enabled the normalization feature in OpenPose so that all keypoint coordinates are located between 0 and 1. We calculated the centroid of the person using the keypoint locations and the Root Mean Square (RMS) of difference in centroid locations of the person in modified and original images for each setting for all the knobs as a measure of accuracy. Figure 4b visually shows the original and modified images after detecting the pose of the pedestrian before and after the application of tuning knobs 1, 2 and 3.

(a)   (b)

Fig. 4. (a) Original and modified images resulting from tuning knobs 2 and 3. *Top left:* original image frame, *Top right:* BGR↔Gray image, *Bottom left:* BGR↔HSV image, *Bottom right:* image modified using blurring filter kernel size of (15, 15) (b) Original and modified images showing the detected pose of the pedestrian from OpenPose. *Top left:* BGR↔Gray image, *Top right:* image modified using blurring filter kernel size of (15, 15), *Bottom left:* BGR↔LAB image, *Bottom right:* image frame with resolution 400×225 (Color figure online)

5.3   Characterizing Image Size Vs. Application Accuracy

We now systematically evaluate the impact of the tuning knobs on image size and application accuracy (TPR for object detection, and RMSE for pose estimation). Figure 5a shows the plot of the True Positive Rate (TPR) of detected objects vs. image size for the object detection application. Note that higher TPR indicates higher accuracy. The relationship between TPR and image size is complex since multiple image size values (obtained from different combinations of knob settings) map to similar TPR values. In Fig. 5a, it is observed that images greater than 400 KB, have maximum TPR above 0.8 and median TPR above 0.7. For images below 400 KB size, we see that the median TPR decreases below 0.6, but the presence of knobs with TPR close to 1.0 makes the images in this size range usable for the object detection application.

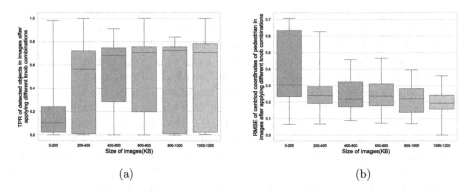

(a)   (b)

Fig. 5. (a) TPR (True Positive Rate) of detected objects in images (from Fig. 4a) when different knob combinations are applied on them vs. image size for MobileNetSSD-object detection benchmark (b) RMS (Root Mean Square) of difference in centroid locations of pedestrians in images (from Fig. 4a) when different knob combinations are applied on them vs. image size for OpenPose-pose estimation benchmark

This key observation enables transmission of smaller sized images with almost similar TPR as the original image from the camera node to the Edge server, in the presence of channel interference. We exploit this observation in the design of the latency controller described in Sect. 6.

A similar design freedom is observed in Fig. 5b where the RMS error in centroid location of keypoints of pedestrians in the OpenPose application is plotted against image size. Note that here lower RMSE indicates higher accuracy. Figure 5b depicts that images in all size ranges have RMSE value as low as <0.1. An important observation from Figs. 5a and 5b is that the design space consists of feasible (infeasible) regions where latency and accuracy specifications are jointly met (unmet).

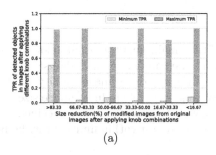
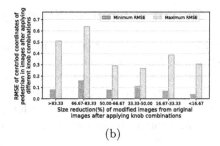

(a)   (b)

Fig. 6. (a) Minimum and maximum values for TPR of detected objects using object detection benchmark in video clips (from CADP dataset) when different knob combinations are applied on them (b) Minimum and maximum values for RMS (Root Mean Square) of difference in centroid locations of pedestrians detected by pose estimation benchmark in video clips (from JAAD dataset) after applying different knob combinations on them. x-axis of both figures plots the percentage size reduction achieved by images extracted from the video clips after modification using tuning knobs

We investigate the broader applicability of the proposed image tuning knobs to the videos in the CADP and JAAD data set described in Sect. 4.1. Figure 6a shows the minimum and maximum values for TPR of detected objects using object detection benchmark in video clips from CADP data set when different knob combinations are applied on them. Figure 6b displays the minimum and maximum values for RMS (Root Mean Square) of difference in centroid

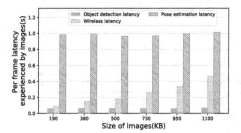

Fig. 7. Different delay components (Wireless latency, Object detection and Pose estimation latency) in the Edge test bed (Fig. 1) plotted against image size

locations of pedestrians detected by pose estimation benchmark in video clips from JAAD dataset after applying different knob combinations on them. x-axis of Fig. 6a and 6b plots the percentage size reduction achieved by images extracted from the video clips after modification using tuning knobs. The plots in Fig. 6 shows the general utility of the proposed image tuning knobs in achieving a range of detection accuracy for different image sizes.

In Fig. 7 we investigate the dependence of the compute latency on the image size. We note that, in contrast to wireless communication latency, for both object detection and pose estimation applications, the compute latency is independent of image size. However, the compute latency dominates in the pose detection application. As mentioned before, the compute latency is an artifact of the relatively lower-end GPU used in this experiment, and will decrease with more powerful hardware.

6   Design of Control Strategy

In this section we describe the algorithm that maintains the application specified image frame transmission latency from the camera to the Edge server in the presence of interference, by automatically tuning the image quality knobs identified in Sect. 5. The control mechanism constructively reduces image size, to match the measured image transfer latency with the target latency specified by the application, while maintaining the accuracy request within limits throughout the operation.

The camera nodes shown in Fig. 1 need to be able to provide image frames within the latency and accuracy levels (TPR or RMSE) requested by the vision applications executing on the Edge server. Since the dependence of application accuracy is complex (see Sect. 5.3), we have two options - (1) Use a sophisticated machine learning model to predict the accuracy and knob combinations for an input image size, or (2) Use a look up table that stores the image size and application accuracy for all knob combinations. We chose the lookup table approach since the total knob combinations of the 5 knobs results in 2500 values, a small number easily stored in memory. These can be initially characterized and quickly looked up using a primary hashtable with the image size as the key, and the candidate accuracies as the value. A secondary hashtable uses the accuracy as the key and the knob settings as the values.

The control algorithm is outlined in the psuedo code shown in Listing 1.

Algorithm 1. Latency control algorithm

   Result: Image quality knob setting

1 latencyTarget;

2 accuracyTarget;

3 errorThreshold;

4 nominalImageSize ← BinSearch(latencyTarget);

5 latencyError ← latencySampled - latencyTarget;

6 **while** *latencyError > errorThreshold* **do**

7 | imageSize = nominalImageSize + K1*latencyError + K2*latencyErrorIntegral;

8 | accuracy ← PrimaryHashTable.lookup(imageSize);

9 | knobSetting ← SecondaryHashTable.lookup(accuracy);

10 | **if** *accuracy > AccuracyTarget* **then**

11 | | return knobSetting;

12 | **else**

13 | | return(No feasible solution);

14 | |

15 | **end**

16 | latencyError ← latencySampled - latencyTarget;

17 **end**

The Edge latency controller running on the camera nodes periodically samples the image transfer latency to verify if it is under the requested limit. The control is implemented in two steps - In Step 1, the error (error and integral of error for Proportional-Integral control) between the observed the the specified latency is used to determine the image size that can potentially satisfy latency requirements. The almost linear dependence of latency on image size (see Sect. 4) facilitates an efficient binary search for the nominal image size. In Step 2, we lookup the primary hashtable with the image size as the key to determine the candidate accuracy values. For the accuracy values that satisfy the application request, the secondary hashtable is used to lookup the knob combinations. The image frames transmitted from camera to Edge node are modified subject to these knob combinations. The latency is measured again at the next sampling interval, and if the error exceeds a preset threshold, Steps 1 and 2 are repeated.

If the application requested latency and accuracy are infeasible, the application is notified. At this point, the application has to decide whether to continue operation with relaxed requirements, or send the notification higher up the stack to the user.

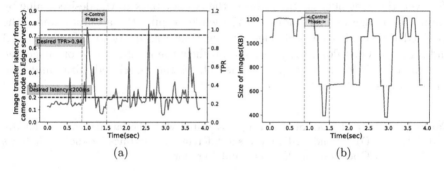

Fig. 8. (a) Latency control and (b) image size reduction during the control phase for MobileNetSSD-Object detection benchmark in presence of channel interference

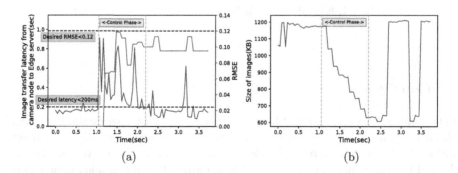

Fig. 9. (a) Latency control and (b) image size reduction during the control phase for OpenPose-Pose estimation benchmark in presence of channel interference

7   Evaluation and Results

We evaluated the control algorithm described in Sect. 6 on the Edge test bed described in Sect. 4. The camera node under test and the peer camera node were kept at a distance of 5 m and 3 m from the access point. For both the MobielNet-SSD and OpenPose benchmarks (see Sect. 5.2), the application request latency was set at less than 200ms. For SSD, TPR was set at greater than 0.94, while for OpenPose the RMSE was set at less than 0.12. Initially, only the camera node under test was transmitting image frames to the Edge server. The controller was able to satisfy these requirements with a median image size of 1 MB for both MobileNetSSD and OpenPose. Note that the resulting latency and accuracy exceed the specifications. To study the effectiveness of the controller when the wireless channel is subject to interference, the peer camera node was turned on to transmit images. Figures 8a and 9a show the control action (latency vs. time). Initially the latency increases due to the interference from the peer camera node. However, the controller is able to bring the latency back to the desired value by tuning the image quality knobs, all the while keeping the accuracy under the specified threshold. The controller settling time was 0.63 s for MobileNetSSD and 1.15 s for OpenPose. Figure 8b and 9b show the resulting plot of image size vs. time for the controller action. Table 1 shows the associated initial and final knob settings.

Table 1. Initial and final knob settings associated with the latency control. R1-R5, C1-C5, K1-K5, D1-D4 and F1-F5 represent different knob settings for knobs 1–5. Rows 1 and 2 are for OpenPose, while rows 3 and 4 are for SSD.

No.	Knob settings	Median image size (KB)	RMSE	TPR
1	R1, C1, K1, D1, F2	1062.3	0.01	-
2	R1, C1, K1, D1, F3	629.9	0.1004	-
3	R1, C1, K2, D1, F4	1049.8	-	1.0
4	R2, C1, K1, D1, F5	652.5	-	1.0

8   Conclusions

In this paper, we demonstrated how latency and accuracy specifications of Edge vision application can be achieved despite the presence of significant latency variations due to interference in the wireless channel. The control knobs are derived from the approximate computing paradigm that a degraded image quality can be tolerated as long as application accuracy requirements are satisfied. We proposed an efficient two-step control algorithm that uses a proportional integral controller, and a hashtable based lookup to dynamically determine the control knob settings based on latancies sampled during operation. Our control approach is scalable since each camera node runs its controller independently. Our experimental results on an Edge test bed with object detection, and human pose estimation machine vision applications show that the proposed controller can correct for latency variations of upto 164% within a settling time of less than 1.15 s.

Future research directions include evaluating the proposed approximate control algorithm on other machine vision applications such as object tracking, and studying the impact on interference as nodes are scaled. Another interesting direction is to study the trade-offs between centralized vs. decentralized control. Unlike the decentralized approach proposed in the paper, centralized control at the Edge server can coordinate transmission between the camera nodes to reduce overall interference, but can potentially be subject to scalability limitations.

References

1. Mobilenet-ssd. https://github.com/chuanqi305/MobileNet-SSD. Accessed 12 Nov 2018
2. Opencv documentation. https://docs.opencv.org. Accessed 08 Nov 2018
3. Ben Khadra, M.A.: An introduction to approximate computing. CoRR abs/1711.06115 (2017). http://arxiv.org/abs/1711.06115
4. Betzel, F., Khatamifard, K., Suresh, H., Lilja, D.J., Sartori, J., Karpuzcu, U.: Approximate communication: techniques for reducing communication bottlenecks in large-scale parallel systems. ACM Comput. Surv. (CSUR) 51(1), 1 (2018)
5. Bonomi, F., Milito, R., Natarajan, P., Zhu, J.: Fog computing: a platform for internet of things and analytics. In: Bessis, N., Dobre, C. (eds.) Big Data and Internet of Things: A Roadmap for Smart Environments. SCI, vol. 546, pp. 169–186. Springer, Cham (2014). https://doi.org/10.1007/978-3-319-05029-4_7
6. Bonomi, F., Milito, R., Zhu, J., Addepalli, S.: Fog computing and its role in the internet of things. In: Proceedings of the First Edition of the MCC Workshop on Mobile Cloud Computing, MCC 2012, pp. 13–16. ACM, New York (2012). https://doi.org/10.1145/2342509.2342513
7. Cao, Z., Simon, T., Wei, S.E., Sheikh, Y.: Realtime multi-person 2D pose estimation using part affinity fields. In: 2017 IEEE Conference on Computer Vision and Pattern Recognition (CVPR) (2017). https://doi.org/10.1109/CVPR.2017.143
8. Chen, C., Choi, J., Gopalakrishnan, K., Srinivasan, V., Venkataramani, S.: Exploiting approximate computing for deep learning acceleration. In: 2018 Design, Automation & Test in Europe Conference & Exhibition, DATE 2018, Dresden, Germany, 19–23 March 2018, pp. 821–826 (2018). https://doi.org/10.23919/DATE.2018.8342119
9. Chiang, M., Zhang, T.: Fog and iot: an overview of research opportunities. IEEE Internet Things J. PP(99), 1 (2016)
10. Ha, K., Chen, Z., Hu, W., Richter, W., Pillai, P., Satyanarayanan, M.: Towards wearable cognitive assistance. In: Proceedings of the 12th Annual International Conference on Mobile Systems, Applications, and Services, MobiSys 2014. pp. 68–81. ACM, New York, (2014). https://doi.org/10.1145/2594368.2594383
11. Howard, A.G., et al.: Mobilenets: Efficient convolutional neural networks for mobile vision applications (2017)

12. Ibrahim, A., Osta, M., Alameh, M., Saleh, M., Chible, H., Valle, M.: Approximate computing methods for embedded machine learning. In: 2018 25th IEEE International Conference on Electronics, Circuits and Systems (ICECS), pp. 845–848. IEEE (2018)
13. Lecun, Y., Bengio, Y., Hinton, G.: Deep learning. Nature **521**(7553), 436–444 (2015)
14. Lee, E.A., et al.: The swarm at the edge of the cloud. IEEE Design Test **31**(3), 8–20 (2014)
15. Liu, W., et al.: SSD: single shot multibox detector. In: Leibe, B., Matas, J., Sebe, N., Welling, M. (eds.) ECCV 2016. LNCS, vol. 9905, pp. 21–37. Springer, Cham (2016). https://doi.org/10.1007/978-3-319-46448-0_2
16. Lu, Y., Chowdhery, A., Kandula, S.: Visflow: a relational platform for efficient large-scale video analytics. Technical report, June 2016. https://www.microsoft.com/en-us/research/publication/visflow-relational-platform-efficient-large-scale-video-analytics/
17. Mittal, S.: A survey of techniques for approximate computing. ACM Comput. Surv. (CSUR) **48**(4), 62 (2016)
18. Pakha, C., Chowdhery, A., Jiang, J.: Reinventing video streaming for distributed vision analytics. In: 10th USENIX Workshop on Hot Topics in Cloud Computing (HotCloud 2018). USENIX Association, Boston, MA (2018). https://www.usenix.org/conference/hotcloud18/presentation/pakha
19. Parag Shah, A., Lamare, J.B., Nguyen-Anh, T., Hauptmann, A.: CADP: a novel dataset for CCTV traffic camera based accident analysis, pp. 1–9 (2018)
20. Rasouli, A., Kotseruba, I., Tsotsos, J.K.: Are they going to cross? A benchmark dataset and baseline for pedestrian crosswalk behavior. In: 2017 IEEE International Conference on Computer Vision Workshops (ICCVW), pp. 206–213 (2017)
21. Sabella, D., Vaillant, A., Kuure, P., Rauschenbach, U., Giust, F.: Mobile-edge computing architecture: the role of mec in the internet of things. IEEE Consum. Electron. Mag. **5**(4), 84–91 (2016)
22. Sapienza, M., Guardo, E., Cavallo, M., Torre, G.L., Leombruno, G., Tomarchio, O.: Solving critical events through mobile edge computing: an approach for smart cities. In: 2016 IEEE International Conference on Smart Computing (SMART-COMP), pp. 1–5, May 2016
23. Satyanarayanan, M., Bahl, P., Caceres, R., Davies, N.: The case for vm-based cloudlets in mobile computing. IEEE Pervasive Comput. **8**(4), 14–23 (2009)
24. Shi, W., Cao, J., Zhang, Q., Li, Y., Xu, L.: Edge computing: vision and challenges. IEEE Internet Things J. **3**(5), 637–646 (2016)
25. Vermesan, O., Friess, P., Guillemin, P., Gusmeroli, S.: Internet of Things Strategic Research Agenda. River Publishers, Alsbjergvej (2011)
26. Zhang, W., Li, S., Liu, L., Jia, Z., Zhang, Y., Raychaudhuri, D.: Hetero-edge: orchestration of real-time vision applications on heterogeneous edge clouds (2019)

Energy-Aware Capacity Provisioning and Resource Allocation in Edge Computing Systems

Tayebeh Bahreini, Hossein Badri, and Daniel Grosu[✉]

Department of Computer Science, Wayne State University, Detroit, USA
{tayebeh.bahreini,hossein.badri,dgrosu}@wayne.edu

Abstract. Energy consumption plays a key role in determining the cost of services in edge computing systems and has a significant environmental impact. Therefore, minimizing the energy consumption in such systems is of critical importance. In this paper, we address the problem of energy-aware optimization of capacity provisioning and resource allocation in edge computing systems. The main goal is to provision and allocate resources such that the net profit of the service provider is maximized, where the profit is the difference between the aggregated users' payments and the total operating cost due to energy consumption. We formulate the problem as a mixed integer linear program and prove that the problem is NP-hard. We develop a heuristic algorithm to solve the problem efficiently. We evaluate the performance of the proposed algorithm by conducting an extensive experimental analysis on problem instances of various sizes. The results show that the proposed algorithm has a very low execution time and is scalable with respect to the number of users in the system.

1 Introduction

Efficient utilization of computing resources has always been an important challenge for service providers, leading to significant efforts on developing solutions, either in the form of new technology or new ways to enhance the efficiency of existing technologies. Edge Computing (EC) is the latest technology developed to mitigate some of the existing challenges in cloud computing. In fact, the high latency in cloud computing systems which stems from the long distance between cloud servers and the end user, triggered the idea of EC systems, that is, bringing computing resources closer to the end user. EC systems are expected to improve the Quality of Service (QoS) by bringing servers closer to the end user, but when it comes to the cost of services, these systems face an important challenge. The operating cost of EC systems is higher than that of the remote clouds, due to the small servers which are distributed across the network. In addition, in EC systems, a larger number of providers compete to provide services at a lower cost, and as a result, obtain a higher market share. It might not be quite easy to lower the investment costs, but when it comes to the operating costs, optimizing the

T. Zhang et al. (Eds.): EDGE 2019, LNCS 11520, pp. 31–45, 2019.
https://doi.org/10.1007/978-3-030-23374-7_3

energy consumption would be a promising way to reduce them. Studies show that about 25% of the operating costs of cloud data centers is attributed to energy consumption [10].

Given these facts, researchers have approached the resource provisioning problem in distributed systems from different perspectives. A variety of algorithms have been proposed to efficiently allocate users' requests to the cloud servers with an emphasis on reducing energy consumption of data centers [4,6,7,18]. Several researchers considered task/workload consolidation as a strategy for reducing the energy consumption [12,15]. Minimizing the total number of active servers is another strategy considered by some researchers. Torres et al. [16] proposed a technique to minimize the total number of active servers without degradation of QoS. Beloglazov et al. [5] and Hameed et al. [11] survey the research on energy-efficient cloud computing systems.

Several studies have focused on computation offloading in EC systems. Trinh et al. [17] studied the impact of computation offloading on energy consumption in EC systems. Chen et al. [8] developed a game theoretic approach for computation offloading in a multi-channel wireless network to minimize the energy consumption of mobile devices and the processing time of applications. Sardellitti et al. [14] and Zhang et al. [19] developed algorithms for decision making on the computational resources and the radio resources to minimize the system energy cost while meeting latency constraints. Bahreini and Grosu [3] designed an iterative matching algorithm for efficient placement of multi-component applications in edge computing systems. These approaches have only focused on resource allocation and did not investigate the capacity provisioning in EC systems.

Anglano et al. [2] developed an algorithm for resource allocation and capacity provisioning in EC systems with the aim of maximizing the profit of the system. To the best of our knowledge, this research is the first work addressing the integrated capacity provisioning and resource allocation in EC systems that takes the energy consumption into account. However, their proposed algorithm is based on solving a mixed-integer linear program which might not be feasible to solve within a reasonable amount of time for large size problems.

Our Contributions. In this paper, we address the capacity provisioning and resource allocation problem in EC systems with the aim of maximizing the net profit of the provider while taking into account the energy consumption of the system. Our main contributions are as follows: (i) develop an energy-aware integrated formulation of the capacity provisioning and resource allocation problem for edge computing systems; (ii) prove that the energy-aware provisioning and resource allocation problem in edge computing systems is NP-hard; (iii) design an efficient heuristic algorithm to solve the problem; and (iv) perform an extensive experimental analysis that shows that the proposed algorithm is scalable with the number of users and produces solutions that are close to optimal.

Organization. The rest of the paper is organized as follows. In Sect. 2, we define the problem and characterize its complexity. In Sect. 3, we describe our proposed heuristic algorithm. In Sect. 4, we define the experimental setup and discuss the experimental results. In Sect. 5, we conclude the paper and propose possible directions for future work.

2   Energy-Aware Capacity Provisioning and Resource Allocation Problem

In this section, we formulate the *Energy-aware Capacity Provisioning and Resource Allocation* (ECPRA) problem in EC systems. We consider an EC system owned and managed by a single provider that aims at maximizing its net profit (i.e., the profit per unit of time). In this system, users' devices generate a high amount of data that needs real-time processing. To guarantee the QoS for requests, the provider deploys a set of powerful computing resources at the edge of the network. However, these resources are limited and the provider is not able to allocate all requests to the edge side. Therefore, some of the requests will be allocated to the cloud side. On the other hand, the operating cost of edge resources is relatively higher than the operating cost of the cloud resources which results in a higher price per unit of resource at the edge. The provider's goal is to allocate resources to users in order to maximize its net profit, which is the total payment of users minus the total operating cost of resources per unit of time.

We denote the edge/cloud levels by ℓ (i.e., $\ell = 1$ for the edge level, and $\ell = 2$ for the cloud level). The system is composed of M^ℓ physical nodes at each level. Users can request D types of resources. For the sake of making the presentation simpler, we assume that $D = 3$, that is, there are three types of resources that a user can request: CPU (cores) ($k = 1$), memory ($k = 2$), and storage ($k = 3$). The capacity of node h at level ℓ for the resource of type k is denoted by C_{hk}^ℓ. We consider N users requesting resources as containers from the provider. The request of user i consists of Q_i containers and is denoted by $R_i = \{r_{i1k}, \ldots, r_{iQ_ik}\}$, where r_{ijk} is the amount of resource of type k requested by user i for container j. As an example, suppose that user i's request is $R_i = \{\{4, 6, 0\}, \{2, 1, 5\}\}$. This means that the number of containers, Q_i, requested by user i, is two ($Q_i = 2$). The first container requires four cores, 6 GB of memory, and no storage, while the second container requires two cores, 1 GB of memory, and 5 GB of storage. The provider allocates a given container to a single node. Also, to have a consistent response time from the physical nodes, the whole request from a user is allocated at either edge or cloud level, but not at both.

Upon receiving the request, the provider decides how to provision resources and allocate the users' requests in order to maximize the total profit, where the profit is the difference between the payments received form the users and the operating cost. We consider that *the operating cost of a node is proportional to the energy consumption of that node* which can be estimated by a linear function of CPU, memory, and disk utilization [13, 20]. Therefore, the energy consumption is captured in the objective function through the operating cost. The *operating cost* (due to energy consumption) of a powered-on node h at level ℓ is given by,

$$E_h^\ell = \delta_h^\ell + \sum_{k=1}^{3} u_{hk}^\ell \cdot \rho_{hk}^\ell \tag{1}$$

where, δ_h^ℓ is the operating cost of node h at level ℓ when it is idle, ρ_{hk}^ℓ is the operating cost of node h for the resource of type k when the resource is fully utilized, and u_{hk}^ℓ is the utilization rate of node h's resource of type k. The utilization u_{hk}^ℓ is given by,

$$u_{hk}^\ell = \frac{1}{C_{hk}^\ell} \sum_{i=1}^{N} \sum_{j=1}^{Q_i} z_{hij}^\ell \cdot r_{ijk} \tag{2}$$

where z_{hij}^ℓ is a binary variable associated with the allocation of container j of user i to node h at level ℓ. The value of this variable is 1, if container j of user i is allocated to node h at level ℓ; and 0, otherwise. Therefore, the *total operating cost* of the system is,

$$E = \sum_{\ell=1}^{2} \sum_{h=1}^{M^\ell} x_h^\ell \cdot \delta_h^\ell + \sum_{\ell=1}^{2} \sum_{h=1}^{M^\ell} \sum_{k=1}^{3} u_{hk}^\ell \cdot \rho_{hk}^\ell \tag{3}$$

where, x_h^ℓ is a binary decision variable associated with the status of node h at level ℓ. Variable x_h^ℓ is 1 if the node is powered on; and 0, otherwise. These decision variables determine how many servers will be turned on by the provider, and therefore represent the capacity provisioning decision.

The provider charges each user a certain amount of money per each unit of time. The amount of money depends on the level that the user's request is allocated and the amount of resources that user requested. Denoting the *unit price* of a resource of type k at level ℓ by π_k^ℓ, the *payment of user i* is defined as,

$$p_i = \sum_{j=1}^{Q_i} \sum_{k=1}^{3} \sum_{\ell=1}^{2} y_i^\ell \cdot \pi_k^\ell \cdot r_{ijk} \tag{4}$$

where, y_i^ℓ is a binary variable, $y_i^\ell = 1$ if user i is allocated at level ℓ; and 0, otherwise. Therefore, we define the *net profit*, Π, of the provider as the aggregated users payments minus the total operating cost of nodes,

$$\Pi = \sum_{i=1}^{N} \sum_{j=1}^{Q_i} \sum_{k=1}^{3} \sum_{\ell=1}^{2} y_i^\ell \cdot \pi_k^\ell \cdot r_{ijk} - \sum_{\ell=1}^{2} \sum_{h=1}^{M^\ell} x_h^\ell \cdot \delta_h^\ell$$
$$- \sum_{i=1}^{N} \sum_{j=1}^{Q_i} \sum_{k=1}^{3} \sum_{\ell=1}^{2} \sum_{h=1}^{M^\ell} z_{hij}^l \cdot \frac{r_{ijk} \cdot \rho_{hk}^\ell}{C_{hk}^\ell} \tag{5}$$

To simplify the equations for profit, we define the following parameters:

$$w_{hij}^\ell = \sum_{k=1}^{3} \frac{r_{ijk} \cdot \rho_{hk}^\ell}{C_{hk}^\ell} \quad \text{and} \quad \eta_i^\ell = \sum_{j=1}^{Q_i} \sum_{k=1}^{3} \pi_k^\ell \cdot r_{ijk} \tag{6}$$

Now, we formulate the *Edge Capacity Provisioning and Resource Allocation* (ECPRA) problem. Table 1 summarizes the notation that we use in our formulation. The mixed-integer linear program (MILP) formulation of ECPRA is as follows,

Table 1. Notation

Notation	Description
N	Number of users
M^ℓ	Number of physical nodes at level ℓ
D	Number of resource types
Q_i	Number of containers requested by user i
r_{ijk}	Amount of resource of type k from container j of user i
C_{hk}^ℓ	Capacity of node h at level l for resource of type k
δ_h^ℓ	Operating cost of node h at level l in idle mode
ρ_{hk}^ℓ	Operating cost of node h at level l for resource of type k fully utilized
π_k^ℓ	Unit price of resource of type k at level ℓ
x_h^ℓ	Binary decision variable; status of node h at level ℓ
z_{hij}^ℓ	Binary decision variable; allocation of container j of user i
y_i^ℓ	Binary decision variable; allocation of user i at level ℓ

ECPRA-MILP:

$$\text{Maximize} \quad \sum_{i=1}^{N} \sum_{\ell=1}^{2} y_i^\ell \cdot \eta_i^\ell - \sum_{\ell=1}^{2} \sum_{h=1}^{M^\ell} x_h^\ell \cdot \delta_h^\ell - \sum_{i=1}^{N} \sum_{j=1}^{Q_i} \sum_{\ell=1}^{2} \sum_{h=1}^{M^\ell} z_{hij}^\ell \cdot \omega_{hij}^\ell \quad (7)$$

subject to:

$$\sum_{i=1}^{N} \sum_{j=1}^{Q_i} z_{hij}^\ell \cdot r_{ijk} \leq x_h^\ell \cdot C_{hk}^\ell \quad \forall h, \forall k, \forall \ell \quad (8)$$

$$y_i^\ell \cdot Q_i \leq \sum_{h=1}^{M^\ell} \sum_{j=1}^{Q_i} z_{hij}^\ell \quad \forall i, \forall \ell \quad (9)$$

$$\sum_{\ell=1}^{2} \sum_{h=1}^{M^\ell} z_{hij}^\ell \leq 1 \quad \forall i, \forall j \quad (10)$$

$$x_h^\ell \in \{0, 1\}, \quad y_i^\ell \in \{0, 1\} \quad \forall h, \forall \ell \quad (11)$$

$$z_{hij}^\ell \in \{0, 1\} \quad \forall i, \forall j, \forall \ell, \forall h \quad (12)$$

Equation (7) is the objective function which is the total net profit of the provider. Constraints (8) ensure that the total allocated resources of each type on node h at level ℓ does not exceed the available capacity of that type of resource. Note that these constraints also determine the mode of the node; if $x_h^\ell = 1$, the corresponding node is on; otherwise, the node is off and no request can be allocated to it. Constraints (9) guarantee that user i is allocated at level ℓ if and only if the whole request of this user is allocated to the nodes situated at level ℓ. Constraints (10) ensure that no container is allocated to more than one node. Finally, constraints (11–12) guarantee the integrality of the decision variables.

2.1 Complexity of ECPRA

We prove that ECPRA is an NP-hard problem, that is, it is not solvable in polynomial time, unless $P = NP$. We prove this claim by showing that a special case of this problem is NP-hard.

Theorem. The ECPRA problem is NP-hard.

Proof. Let us consider a special case of ECPRA in which there is only one user in the system, and there exists only one level of resources. We call this problem ECPRA-S. We show that ECPRA-S is an NP-hard problem. Then, we conclude that ECPRA, which is the general case of ECPRA-S, is NP-hard as well.

From Eq. (7), the objective of ECPRA-S for user i at level ℓ is,

$$\text{Maximize} \quad y_i^\ell \cdot \eta_i^\ell - \sum_{h=1}^{M^\ell} x_h^\ell \cdot \delta_h^\ell - \sum_{j=1}^{Q_i} \sum_{h=1}^{M^\ell} z_{hij}^\ell \cdot \omega_{hij}^\ell \tag{13}$$

Since there is only one user in the system, the first term in the objective function (η_i^ℓ) has a fixed value, that is, it does not have any effects on the solution. Therefore, we can ignore it. Furthermore, for our purpose, we convert the objective from maximization to minimization. Since i and ℓ have a fixed value, for the sake of readability, we define binary variables $\bar{x}_h$ and $\bar{y}_{hj}$, where $\bar{x}_h = x_h^\ell$ and $\bar{z}_{hj} = z_{hij}^\ell$. We also define parameters, $\bar{\delta}_h = \delta_h^\ell$, $\bar{\omega}_{hj} = \omega_{hij}^\ell$, $\bar{r}_{jk} = r_{ijk}$ and $\bar{C}_{hk} = C_{hk}^\ell$. Thus, we can formulate ECPRA-S as,

$$\text{Minimize} \quad \sum_{h=1}^{M^\ell} \bar{x}_h \cdot \bar{\delta}_h + \sum_{j=1}^{Q_i} \sum_{h=1}^{M^\ell} \bar{z}_{hj} \cdot \bar{\omega}_{hj} \tag{14}$$

subject to:

$$\sum_{j=1}^{Q_i} \bar{z}_{hj} \cdot \bar{r}_{jk} \leq \bar{x}_h \cdot \bar{C}_{hk} \quad \forall h, \forall k \tag{15}$$

$$\sum_{h=1}^{M^\ell} \bar{z}_{hj} \leq 1 \quad \forall j \tag{16}$$

$$\bar{x}_h \in \{0, 1\} \quad \forall h \tag{17}$$

$$\bar{z}_{hj} \in \{0, 1\} \quad \forall h, \forall j \tag{18}$$

We observe that ECPRA-S is the general case of the Capacitated Facility Location (CFL) problem [9], where instead of having a single type of goods, each facility provides different types of goods. In fact, in CFL, there is a set of facilities (nodes), each facility provides a single type of goods (resources) with a limited capacity (Constraints (15)). There is also a set of clients (set of containers), and a client j has a demand, $\bar{r}_{jk}$. The whole demand of a client must be assigned to a single facility (Constraints (16)). Each facility has a fixed cost to be opened, $\bar{\delta}_h$. Satisfying the demand of each client from each facility has a different cost, $\bar{\omega}_{hj}$. The goal is to select a subset of facilities to open, in order to minimize the sum of the cost of the assignment, plus the sum of facilities' opening cost (Eq. (14)). CFL is a well-known NP-hard problem [9]. Since ECPRA-S is a generalization of CFL, ECPRA-S is NP-hard as well. Furthermore, ECPRA is a generalization of ECPRA-S. Therefore, ECPRA is an NP-hard problem.

3   A Greedy Algorithm for **ECPRA**

ECPRA is NP-hard and therefore, it is not solvable in polynomial time, unless $P = NP$. We give up on optimality and develop a greedy algorithm, called G-ECPRA, that provides a suboptimal solution to ECPRA in polynomial time. Our greedy algorithm is an iterative algorithm; and in each iteration, the allocation of only one user is determined. In fact, in each iteration of the algorithm, a user that maximizes the revenue of the system is selected, and then, the algorithm finds an allocation for that user that minimizes the operating cost of the system.

   The proposed algorithm for solving the ECPRA problem is given in Algorithm 1. The algorithm has as input the vector of users' requests and the capacity of the nodes at each level, and determines the allocation of these requests. The output of the algorithm consists of the profit of the provider, Π, and the allocation matrices $X = \{x_h^\ell\}$, $Y = \{y_i^\ell\}$, and $Z = \{z_{hij}^\ell\}$.

   First, G-ECPRA initializes the allocation matrices X, Y, and Z, and the status matrix $S = \{s_h^\ell\}$ (Line 1). The status matrix indicates the status of the nodes after the last iteration of the algorithm, that is, $s_h^\ell = 0$ if node h at level ℓ is turned on, and $s_h^\ell = 1$ if that node is off. Initially, this matrix is set to 1, that is, no node is selected to be turned on. G-ECPRA then determines the average revenue, Γ_i, that each user can bring to the system (Lines 2–3). It sorts users in non-increasing order of Γ_i (Line 4). Then, in each iteration of the algorithm, an unallocated user with the maximum Γ_i is chosen in order to maximize the revenue of the provider. In this step, Algorithm G-CFL is called twice to determine the possible allocations for the current user at both the edge level and the cloud level (Lines 6–7). G-CFL gets the request of the user, the current capacity at level ℓ, and the status of nodes, S, and finds an allocation for the user at level ℓ such that the operating cost is minimized. In fact, G-CFL tries to find a solution for ECPRA-S (we will explain this algorithm in more details later). $\bar{X}^\ell$ and $\bar{Z}^\ell$ are temporary matrices corresponding to the output matrices $\bar{X}$ and $\bar{Z}$ obtained by G-CFL for the current user at level ℓ, and $cost^\ell$ is the cost of allocating the current user at level ℓ.

   G-ECPRA determines the possible contribution to the profit by the current user, $\Pi^\ell = \eta_i^\ell - cost^\ell$ (Line 8). Then, the algorithm picks the level that yields the maximum profit (Line 9). If the profit at this level is positive, it means that G-CFL has found a feasible allocation for this user. In this case, the allocation matrices X, Y, Z, and the profit of the system are updated (Lines 10–16). If the

---

Algorithm 1. G-ECPRA

Input: Users' requests: $\{R_1, \ldots, R_N\}$
        Nodes' capacity: $C = \{C_{hk}^{\ell}\}$
1: $\Pi \leftarrow 0,\ X \leftarrow 0,\ Y \leftarrow 0,\ Z \leftarrow 0,\ S \leftarrow 1$
2: **for** $i = 1 \ldots N$ **do**
3:     $\Gamma_i \leftarrow \sum_{j=1}^{Q_i} \sum_{k=1}^{3} \frac{(\pi_k^1 + \pi_k^2)}{2} \cdot r_{ijk}$
4: sort users in non-increasing order of Γ_i
5: **for** $i = 1 \ldots N$ **do**
6:     **for** $\ell = 1 \ldots 2$ **do**
7:         $\{\bar{X}^{\ell}, \bar{Z}^{\ell}, cost^{\ell}\} \leftarrow$ G-CFL$(R_i, C^{\ell}, S^{\ell})$
8:         $\Pi^{\ell} \leftarrow \eta_i^{\ell} - cost^{\ell}$
9:     $\ell^* \leftarrow \text{argmax}_{\ell \in \{1,2\}} \Pi^{\ell}$
10:    **if** $\Pi^{\ell^*} > 0$ **then**
11:        $\Pi \leftarrow \Pi + \Pi^{\ell^*}$
12:        $y_i^{\ell^*} \leftarrow 1$
13:        **for** $h \in M^{\ell^*}$ **do**
14:            $x_h^{\ell^*} \leftarrow \bar{x}_h^{\ell^*}$
15:            **for** $j = 1 \ldots Q_i$ **do**
16:                $z_{hij}^{\ell^*} \leftarrow \bar{z}_{hj}^{\ell^*}$

Output: X, Y, Z, Π

---

profit is negative, it means that G-CFL has not found a feasible allocation for the user. Therefore, the allocation matrices will not be updated. This procedure is repeated until all users are considered.

The G-CFL algorithm, presented in Algorithm 2, finds an allocation for user i at level ℓ with the minimum operating cost. In fact, G-CFL solves the ECPRA-S problem. However, in the problem that G-CFL solves, some nodes might have been turned on due to the allocation of the previous users. Therefore, if any container of the current user is allocated on these nodes, no fixed cost δ_h^{ℓ}, will be added to the system.

G-CFL has as inputs the request of user i, the current capacity of the nodes at level ℓ, and the status matrix. It determines the allocation for user i. The output of G-CFL is the cost of allocating user i at level ℓ, and the allocation matrices $\bar{Z} = \{\bar{z}_{jk}\}$ and $\bar{X} = \{\bar{x}_h\}$.

First, G-CFL creates a set of unallocated containers, $\mathcal{R}$. Initially, $\mathcal{R}$ contains all user i's containers (Line 2). Then, the algorithm computes the cost of assigning each container on each node. For this purpose, function available is called (Line 6) to check whether node h has enough capacity for container j. If there are enough resources, then the cost of the assignment is given by $s_h^{\ell} \cdot \delta_h^{\ell} + w_{hij}^{\ell}$. Otherwise, the cost of the assignment is infinity, which means that the assignment is infeasible (Lines 4–9).

Then, G-CFL assigns containers to the nodes iteratively. In each iteration, it chooses a pair of node and container (h^*, j^*) that has the minimum value of assignment cost (Line 11). If $cost_{h^*j^*}$ is not infinity, it means that assigning container j^* to node h^* at level ℓ^* is feasible. In this case, the algorithm updates

Algorithm 2. G-CFL

Input: Request of user i; $R_i = \{r_{ijk}\}$
Nodes' capacities at level ℓ; $C^\ell = \{C^\ell_{kh}\}$
Status of nodes at level ℓ; $S^\ell = \{s^\ell_h\}$

1: $\Pi \leftarrow 0$, $\bar{X} \leftarrow 0$, $\bar{Z} \leftarrow 0$
2: $\mathcal{R} \leftarrow \{1, \ldots, Q_i\}$
3: $\bar{C} \leftarrow C^\ell$
4: **for** each $j \in \mathcal{R}$ **do**
5:     **for** $h = 1, \ldots, M^\ell$ **do**
6:         **if** available$(\widehat{C}_h, j)$ **then**
7:             $cost_{hj} \leftarrow \bar{x}^\ell_h \cdot \delta^\ell_h + \omega'_{hj}$
8:         **else**
9:             $cost_{hj} \leftarrow \infty$
10: **while** $\mathcal{R} \neq \emptyset$ **do**
11:     $(h^*, j^*) \leftarrow \text{argmin}_{(h,j)}(cost_{hj})$
12:     **if** $cost_{h^*j^*} \neq \infty$ **then**
13:         $\bar{C}_{h^*} \leftarrow \bar{C}_{h^*} - r_{ij}$
14:         $\bar{z}_{h^*j^*} \leftarrow 1$
15:         $\bar{x}_{h^*} \leftarrow 1$
16:         $cost \leftarrow cost + cost_{h^*j^*}$
17:         remove j^* from $\mathcal{R}$
18:         **for** each $j \in \mathcal{R}$ **do**
19:             **if** available$(\bar{C}_{h^*}, j)$ **then**
20:                 $cost_{h^*j} \leftarrow \omega'_{h^*j}$
21:             **else**
22:                 $cost_{h^*j} \leftarrow \infty$
23:     **else**
24:         $cost \leftarrow \infty$
25:         **break;**
26: **if** $cost \neq \infty$ **then**
27:     **for** $h = 1, \ldots, M^\ell$ **do**
28:         $C^\ell_h \leftarrow \bar{C}_h$
29:         **if** $\bar{x}_h = 1$ **then**
30:             $s^\ell_h \leftarrow 0$

Output: $\bar{X}$, $\bar{Z}$, $cost$

---

the capacity of the node, temporarily. Matrices $\bar{X}$ and $\bar{Z}$ and the cost of the system are also updated (Lines 12–16). Then, the algorithm removes container j^* from $\mathcal{R}$ (Line 17). After that, it updates the cost of assigning each remaining container to node $S^\ell_{h^*}$. Since this node is on now, the fixed cost must not be considered in any other assignments of this node. The algorithm also checks if by this assignment, there are not enough resources for a container, then the cost of the further assignment is set to infinity (Lines 19–22). If the cost of assignment for (h^*, j^*) is infinity, it means that the minimum assignment cost is infinity. Therefore, the algorithm could not find a feasible assignment for this container and any other containers. Thus, it sets the total assignment cost to infinity, exits from the loop, and does not continue finding allocations for other containers (Lines 23–26). Outside the loop, the algorithm checks the value of *cost*. If it is not infinity, the allocation matrix, status matrix, and capacity are updated (Lines 26–30).

We now analyze the time complexity of the algorithm. In the analysis we use the following notation: $M = \max_\ell M^\ell$ and $Q = \max_i Q_i$. In G-CFL, the initialization (Lines 1–3) takes $\mathcal{O}(DMQ)$. The while loop of G-CFL takes $\mathcal{O}((M + D)Q^2)$. Since D (the number of resource types) is small compared to M and Q, the time complexity of G-CFL is $\mathcal{O}(MQ^2)$. The most time consuming part of G-ECPRA is the call to G-CFL for each user and for each level. Therefore, the time complexity of G-ECPRA is $\mathcal{O}(NMQ^2)$.

4   Experimental Results

In this section, we present an experimental analysis of the performance of our proposed algorithm, G-ECPRA. We compare the performance of G-ECPRA with the optimal solution obtained by solving ECPRA-MILP with CPLEX [1]. Then, we investigate the scalability of G-ECPRA for large size instances. In the following, we describe the experimental setup and analyze the experimental results.

4.1   Experimental Setup

We generate several problem instances with different values for the number of users, N, the number of resource types, D, and the amount of resources requested by each user, r_{ijk}. In the first set of experiments, we compare the performance of G-ECPRA with that of the CPLEX solver. Since the CPLEX solver cannot solve large size problem instances, we perform this analysis on relatively small size problem instances. We assume that there are a few nodes available at the edge level and the cloud level ($M^1 = 5$, $M^2 = 10$). For these problem instances, the number of users varies from 10 to 100, and there are four types of resources, i.e., CPU, memory, storage, and bandwidth. The value of r_{ijk} is chosen from a uniform distribution $U[0, RB]$, where RB is an upper bound for r_{ijk}.

Since the objective of ECPRA-MILP is to maximize the profit, we generate instances according to a metric called *price to cost ratio* (*PCR*). This metric is defined as the ratio of the average price per unit of resource to the average cost per unit of resource:

$$PCR = \frac{\sum_{k=1}^{3} \sum_{\ell=1}^{2} \sum_{h=1}^{M^\ell} C_{kh}^\ell \cdot \pi_k^\ell}{\sum_{\ell=1}^{2} \sum_{h=1}^{M^\ell} (\delta_h^\ell + \sum_{k=1}^{3} C_{kh}^\ell \cdot \rho_{kh}^\ell)} \tag{19}$$

Table 2 shows the probability distributions used to generate the parameters in our experiments. We denote by U$[x, y]$ the uniform distribution on the interval $[x, y]$. To generate problem instances with different values of PCR, the price per unit of each type of resources is drawn from different distributions.

Table 2. Simulation parameters

Param	Distribution	Param	Distribution
C_{hk}^1	$U[1, 300]$	π_k^1	$PCR \approx 1 : U[1, 6]$
C_{hk}^2	$U[30, 300]$		$PCR \approx 2 : U[3, 10]$
Q_i	$U[1, 5]$		$PCR \approx 7 : U[10, 35]$
r_{ijk}	$U[0, RB]$		$PCR \approx 20 : U[40, 120]$
δ_h^1	$U[5, 50]$	π_k^2	$PCR \approx 1 : U[1, 3]$
δ_h^2	$U[1, 40]$		$PCR \approx 2 : U[1, 5]$
ρ_{kh}^1	$U[1, 10]$		$PCR \approx 7 : U[3, 20]$
ρ_{kh}^2	$U[1, 5]$		$PCR \approx 20 : U[10, 80]$

The performance of G-ECPRA is evaluated by computing the profit ratio, Π^r, which is the ratio of the value of the solution obtained by G-ECPRA, denoted by Π, and that of the optimal solution obtained by CPLEX, denoted by Π^*, i.e., $\Pi^r = \frac{\Pi}{\Pi^*}$.

In the second set of experiments, we investigate the scalability of G-ECPRA for large size problem instances. We consider a system with 50 servers at the edge level, and 100 servers at the cloud level ($M^1 = 50$, $M^2 = 100$). There are four types of resources, and the number of users ranges from 100 to 1500.

The G-ECPRA algorithm is implemented in C++ and the experiments are conducted on an Intel 1.6 GHz Core i5 system with 8 GB RAM. For solving G-ECPRA-MILP, we use the CPLEX 12 solver provided by IBM ILOG CPLEX optimization studio for academics initiative [1].

4.2 Experimental Analysis

We first investigate the effects of the number of users on the performance of G-ECPRA. For each value of the number of users, we generate two sets of instances with different values of PCR. In these problem instances, all parameters are identical except π_k^ℓ. The value of π_k^ℓ is chosen according to Table 2, such that in the first set, $PCR \approx 2$, and in the second set, $PCR \approx 20$. For these problem instances, $RB \approx 6$.

Figure 1a shows the execution time for each instance. We observe that for each number of users, the running time of CPLEX for an instance with $PCR \approx 20$ is less than the instance with $PCR \approx 2$. The reason behind this is that when the PCR is high, the effect of the energy cost of servers on the profit of the system is not very significant. Thus, the main problem is to decide only on how to place the requests of each user, either at the edge or at the cloud level, in order to maximize the total payments. Therefore, the CPLEX solver can solve the problem faster than the case in which we have a balance between cost and the price of each unit of resources.

Another observation from Fig. 1a is with respect to the impact of the number of users on the running time. The running time of CPLEX (represented in the

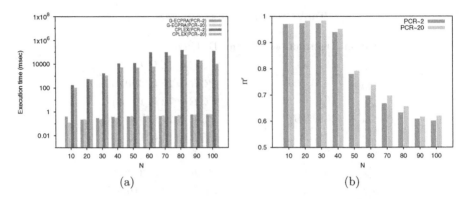

Fig. 1. The effect of PCR on the execution time and profit ratio (small-size instances)

figure using a logarithmic scale) increases exponentially, while that of G-ECPRA increases linearly. Figure 1b shows the profit ratio for each of these instances. As we observe, the profit ratio for instances with $PCR \approx 20$ is higher than that for the instances with $PCR \approx 2$. The reason behind this observation is that with $PCR \approx 20$, minimizing the cost is not so important and the main focus is on maximizing the total payment. Therefore, G-ECPRA, which decomposes the main problem into two subproblems obtains solutions that are not far from solutions of the main problem. Another observation from Fig. 1b is that for both instances, by increasing the number of users, the profit ratio decreases. Since the capacity of the nodes is identical for all instances, by increasing the number of users in the system, the allocation becomes more competitive and it becomes harder to decide how to allocate resources in order to maximize the profit. However, the solution obtained by G-ECPRA is good. For $N = 10$ the profit ratio is about 0.95 while for $N = 100$, it is about 0.6, which is still reasonable.

Next, we analyze the effects of the number of users on the performance of the algorithm. But this time, our analysis is based on two sets of problem instances with different values of the request bound, RB. In fact, we investigate the effects of RB on the quality of solutions. In the first set, each container has at most one unit of each type of resources ($RB = 1$), while in the second set, each container can contain up to eight units of each type of resources ($RB = 8$). For these instances, $PCR \approx 2$. Figure 2a shows the running time of CPLEX and G-ECPRA for each instance. We observe that the running time of G-ECPRA does not change dramatically and is less than 1 ms for all instances. But the running time of CPLEX increases by increasing RB, and for some instances, it exceeds 2050 ms. The reason behind this behavior is that the complexity of the problem increases when each container contains more than one unit of each type of resources. Figure 2b shows that the profit ratio decreases when RB increases. Since by increasing RB, the complexity of the problem increases, the solution obtained by G-ECPRA is farther from the optimal solution than in the case with

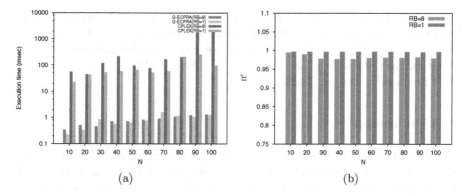

(a)   (b)

Fig. 2. The effect of the request size bound, RB, on the execution time and profit ratio (small-size instances)

smaller values of RB. However, the quality of solutions is still very good (the profit ratio is about 0.98).

In the next set of experiments, we investigate the performance of the algorithm for *large-scale problem instances*. We define two sets of instances with $PCR \approx 1$ and $PCR \approx 7$, respectively. Because for these sets of problem instances the size of problem is large, the CPLEX is unable to obtain the optimal solution in reasonable amount of time. Figure 3a shows the running time of our algorithm for these two instances. As we observe, by increasing the number of users, the running time of our algorithm also increases, but the increase is linear. Even for these large instances, the running time of our algorithm is under 800 ms, thus, making it suitable for deployment in EC systems.

Since, the CPLEX solver is unable to solve these large size problem instances in a reasonable amount of time, we cannot compare the profit obtained by G-ECPRA with that of CPLEX. Figure 3b shows the profit ratio between the profit

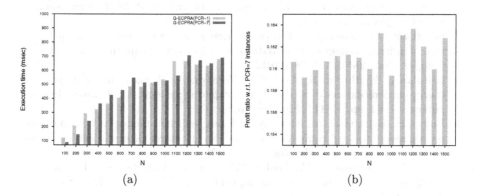

(a)   (b)

Fig. 3. The effect of PCR on the execution time and profit ratio with respect to $PCR \approx 7$ instances (large-size instances)

obtained for instances with $PCR \approx 1$ to the profit obtained for instances with $PCR \approx 7$. We observe that in all cases this ratio is about 0.16 which is very close to the ratio between the PCR of the two instance sets. This indicates that our algorithm has a stable behavior and that the value of PCR does not significantly affect the performance of the algorithm.

5   Conclusion

There is an increasing concern about the energy consumption in edge computing systems, both from the perspective of the environmental impact as well as business competitiveness. In this paper, we proposed an energy-conscious approach for the capacity provisioning and resource allocation problem in edge computing systems. We proposed an MILP formulation of the problem and proved that the problem is NP-hard. In order to solve the problem efficiently, we proposed a heuristic algorithm and analyzed its performance. Our experimental analysis on different sizes and various configurations of the problem showed that the proposed greedy algorithm is competitive with the CPLEX solver in terms of both the computational time and the quality of solutions.

In future work, we plan to develop energy-aware auction based mechanisms for the capacity provisioning and resource planning in edge computing systems. Also, we plan to take the uncertainty of demands into account in the energy-aware capacity provisioning and resource allocation in edge computing systems.

References

1. IBM ILOG CPLEX V12.1 user's manual (2009)
2. Anglano, C., Canonico, M., Guazzone, M.: Profit-aware resource management for edge computing systems. In: Proceedings of the 1st International Workshop on Edge Systems, Analytics and Networking, pp. 25–30. ACM (2018)
3. Bahreini, T., Grosu, D.: Efficient placement of multi-component applications in edge computing systems. In: Proceedings of the 2nd ACM/IEEE Symposium on Edge Computing, pp. 5:1–5:11 (2017)
4. Beloglazov, A., Abawajy, J., Buyya, R.: Energy-aware resource allocation heuristics for efficient management of data centers for cloud computing. Future Gener. Comput. Syst. **28**(5), 755–768 (2012)
5. Beloglazov, A., Buyya, R., Lee, Y.C., Zomaya, A.: A taxonomy and survey of energy-efficient data centers and cloud computing systems. In: Advances in Computers, vol. 82, pp. 47–111. Elsevier (2011)
6. Buyya, R., Beloglazov, A., Abawajy, J.: Energy-efficient management of data center resources for cloud computing: a vision, architectural elements, and open challenges. arXiv preprint arXiv:1006.0308 (2010)
7. Chase, J.S., Anderson, D.C., Thakar, P.N., Vahdat, A.M., Doyle, R.P.: Managing energy and server resources in hosting centers. ACM SIGOPS Oper. Syst. Rev. **35**(5), 103–116 (2001)
8. Chen, X., Jiao, L., Li, W., Fu, X.: Efficient multi-user computation offloading for mobile-edge cloud computing. IEEE/ACM Trans. Netw. **5**, 2795–2808 (2016)

9. Garey, M.R., Johnson, D.S.: Computers and Intractability, A Guide to the Theory of NP-Completeness, vol. 29. WH Freeman, New York (2002)
10. Greenberg, A., Hamilton, J., Maltz, D.A., Patel, P.: The cost of a cloud: research problems in data center networks. ACM SIGCOMM Comput. Commun. Rev. **39**(1), 68–73 (2008)
11. Hameed, A., et al.: A survey and taxonomy on energy efficient resource allocation techniques for cloud computing systems. Computing **98**(7), 751–774 (2016)
12. Lee, Y.C., Zomaya, A.Y.: Energy efficient utilization of resources in cloud computing systems. J. Supercomput. **60**(2), 268–280 (2012)
13. Rivoire, S., Ranganathan, P., Kozyrakis, C.: A comparison of high-level full-system power models. HotPower **8**(2), 32–39 (2008)
14. Sardellitti, S., Scutari, G., Barbarossa, S.: Joint optimization of radio and computational resources for multicell mobile-edge computing. IEEE Trans. Signal Inf. Process. Netw. **1**(2), 89–103 (2015)
15. Srikantaiah, S., Kansal, A., Zhao, F.: Energy aware consolidation for cloud computing. In: Proceedings of the 2008 Conference on Power Aware Computing and Systems, San Diego, California, vol. 10, pp. 1–5 (2008)
16. Torres, J., Carrera, D., Hogan, K., Gavaldà, R., Beltran, V., Poggi, N.: Reducing wasted resources to help achieve green data centers. In: Proceedings IEEE International Symposium on Parallel and Distributed Processing, pp. 1–8. IEEE (2008)
17. Trinh, H., et al.: Energy-aware mobile edge computing for low-latency visual data processing. In: Proceedings of the 5th IEEE International Conference on Future Internet of Things and Cloud, pp. 128–133 (2017)
18. Verma, A., Ahuja, P., Neogi, A.: pMapper: power and migration cost aware application placement in virtualized systems. In: Issarny, V., Schantz, R. (eds.) Middleware 2008. LNCS, vol. 5346, pp. 243–264. Springer, Heidelberg (2008). https://doi.org/10.1007/978-3-540-89856-6_13
19. Zhang, K., et al.: Energy-efficient offloading for mobile edge computing in 5G heterogeneous networks. IEEE Access **4**, 5896–5907 (2016)
20. Zhang, Q., Zhani, M.F., Zhang, S., Zhu, Q., Boutaba, R., Hellerstein, J.L.: Dynamic energy-aware capacity provisioning for cloud computing environments. In: Proceedings of the 9th International Conference on Autonomic Computing, pp. 145–154 (2012)

Stackelberg Game-Theoretic Spectrum Allocation for QoE-Centric Wireless Multimedia Communications

Krishna Murthy Kattiyan Ramamoorthy$^{(\boxtimes)}$, Wei Wang, and Kazem Sohraby

Department of Computer Science, San Diego State University,
San Diego, CA 92182, USA
{kkattiyanramam8285,wwang,ksohraby}@sdsu.edu

Abstract. Multimedia Quality of Experience (QoE) is a predominant factor that drives customer satisfaction and user experience in the future wireless networks. This paper proposes a Stackelberg game theoretic spectrum allocation approach for QoE-centric wireless multimedia communication rather than the traditional data traffic. Here, we introduce the cost of utilizing the spectrum as a factor in the utility of the service provider and the client device. Both service provider and client devices are assumed rational and selfishly look to maximize their utility in a non-cooperative manner. Stackelberg game is used to formulate the interaction between the service provider and the client device, and to derive the Nash Equilibrium for the utility maximization problem. The paper proves existence of a Stackelberg game solution such that the utility of both client device and the service provider is maximized. The simulation results demonstrate that QoE and fairness can be achieved by the proposed game-theoretic spectrum allocation scheme.

Keywords: QoE/QoS resource allocation · Game theory ·
Stackelberg game · Wireless multimedia communications

1 Introduction

The mobile and wireless communication is one of the most rapidly growing technologies. The wireless data traffic is expected to grow 1000-fold by year 2020 and more likely to grow to 10,000-fold by 2030 [1]. Multimedia and video packets constitute the largest share of data traffic over the Internet. With increasing number of Internet-ready devices and the demand for multimedia data, the network becomes congested and the spectrum turn out to be a valuable resource. A good solution for multimedia streaming over the Internet would be to maximize the utilization of the available spectrum, have the capability to adjust video bit rates to varying wireless channel and provide seamless Quality of Experience (QoE) to the user. For example, Dynamic Adaptive Streaming over HTTP (DASH) standard has been proposed by the Moving Picture Experts Group (MPEG)

© Springer Nature Switzerland AG 2019
T. Zhang et al. (Eds.): EDGE 2019, LNCS 11520, pp. 46–58, 2019.
https://doi.org/10.1007/978-3-030-23374-7_4

of International Standardization Organization (ISO)/International Electro technical Commission (IEC) in 2011 [2]. MPEG DASH is a multimedia delivery technology that aims at transporting the best quality content with the fewest dropouts and least possible buffering. Internet-based video delivery today has widely adopted DASH as it provides less latency for a given bandwidth and can be deployed on top of the existing infrastructure, utilizing transport layer protocol (TCP) and the application layer protocol (HTTP) [3,4].

This paper proposes a Stackelberg game-theoretic mechanism for spectrum allocation for the multimedia packets transmitted over the wireless networks as shown in Fig. 1. In this model, the interaction between the service provider and the client is considered as a Stackelberg game, where the SP (Service Provider) makes an announcement for the spectrum cost and then the client decides the quantity of spectrum to request for allocation.

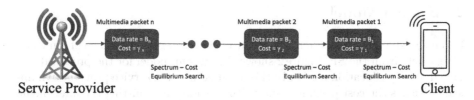

Fig. 1. Interaction between service provider and client in proposed scheme.

The client device aims to maximize its QoE by requesting as much spectrum blocks as possible for a given channel condition and the video description profile (e.g., display resolution, codec support). The service provider, being aware of the channel condition, decides the cost charged for the spectrum blocks for each multimedia packet. The essential questions are: *What should be the suitable cost factor charged by the SP, such that their net utility is maximized? How much spectrum should the client device request for the given cost such that its QoE is maximized?* In this paper, we propose an algorithm that determines the optimal values for the spectrum size and cost. This algorithm is derived by translating the system model into a game-theoretical QoE maximization problem.

Game-theoretic models have been proposed in the past for non-cooperative wireless communications. For example, Nash Equilibrium for multimedia relay communication was analyzed [5], a game for power selection based on the distortion reduction per frame was proposed and equilibrium was achieved [6]. Several game solutions have been developed to address the issues in Dynamic spectrum sharing over cognitive radio [7,8]. In one study, [7], the game is defined between the secondary users and solved for the optimization problem between the secondary users who are competing to maximize their utilities by sharing the spectrum. Another study by Huang and Wang [8], proposes a refunding mechanism in spectrum sharing network where the primary user provides refund to the secondary user if the promised QoS is not achieved. Researchers also propose a cooperative game model to allocate the bandwidth between various users for

DASH [9]. This model assumes the players to be cooperative in order to maximize the spectrum allocated to them. However, in reality, the client devices are bandwidth hungry and selfish. Other research have been performed extensively on resource allocation, QoE optimization or attaining the utility Equilibrium for wireless multimedia communications [14,15]. In the proposed work, we assume the end users to be rational and selfish. We have derived the Nash equilibrium for a single user – single service provider scenario which can be easily extended to a multi-user scenario.

The rest of the paper is organized as follows: Sect. 2 presents the utility models of the SP and the client device. In Sect. 3, we define the utility models as a two-stage Stackelberg game and determine the Nash equilibrium of the game. Simulation results for the proposed game theory model is presented in Sect. 4 and we conclude the paper in Sect. 5.

2   System Model

In multimedia communication, the client device requests a sequence of multimedia packets from the SP. Figure 2 shows the system model for the proposed last mile dynamic allocation model. In this architecture, the service provider dynamically decides the cost per unit bandwidth γ before transmitting the multimedia packets. The service provider has several copies of the requested data with different multimedia profiles obtained from the server. This gives the client device the flexibility to determine the bit rates for every subsequent frame. The client device then determines the amount of bandwidth B to request for given spectrum cost γ. The multimedia QoE achieved by the client is determined by the amount of bandwidth requested. If the client requests high bandwidth, the SP helps transmit the premium content and if the client requests lower bandwidth, the SP transmits regular content.

In this section, we define the utilities of the client and the base station. We use the terms service provider and base station interchangeably. We also use the term client and end-user interchangeably in the rest of this paper.

2.1   Utility of the Client (End-User)

The client requests data from the service provider over the wireless channel. The utility of the client is defined as the income generated from user satisfaction such as the multimedia QoE, minus the payment for service provider's service. The capacity of the wireless channel can be given by the Shannon–Hartley theorem.

$$C = B \, log_2 \left(1 + \frac{p}{\sigma} \right) \tag{1}$$

where B is the total amount of bandwidth allocated to client, and p and σ represent the signal power and noise power in the communication channel. In this paper, we assume that the transmission and the noise power do not change during the data transmission.

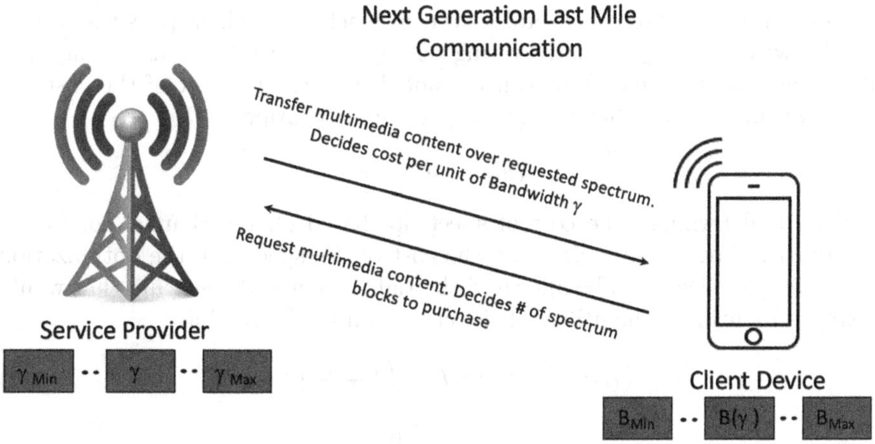

Fig. 2. System model - spectrum allocation in QoE centric wireless multimedia communications.

The utility obtained through the wireless channel can be formulated as the logarithmic function of allocated resource, [10], and it is given by:

$$QoE = \alpha \, log \left(1 + \theta \, B \, log_2 \left(1 + \frac{p}{\sigma}\right)\right) \qquad (2)$$

where α is the payoff parameter and the currency gain for the logarithmic QoE. The packet transmitted over the wireless channel comprises of the protocol overhead and the error control bits apart from the payload information as shown in Table 1 below. The percentage (%) of payload bits per transmission θ is multiplied with the bandwidth term of the QoE equation above as only those bits contribute to the actual QoE.

Table 1. Overhead in wireless communication protocols

Protocol stack	Overhead (HTTP DASH)
Transport layer	TCP (32 bytes)
Network layer	IP (20 bytes)
Datalink layer	Ethernet (14 bytes)/Wi-MAX (6 bytes)
Interframe gap	12 bytes
Preamble	8 bytes
CRC/Error control	4 bytes
Average payload	~576 bytes
Channel utilization (θ)	~50%

The link utilization of the client device would be higher for higher bit rates due to the larger payload. Therefore, to maximize its QoE, the client device will look forward in buying several spectrum blocks. The client pays the service provider with ψ_{Client_SP} for delivering quality of service by transmitting data with requested spectrum. This can be modeled as the product of the cost per unit bandwidth γ and the amount of spectrum allocation B.

$$\psi_{Client\_SP} = \gamma B \tag{3}$$

The SP determines the cost of spectrum based on the channel conditions and spectrum availability. Knowing the cost of the spectrum, the optimization on the client devices is to be allocated the right amount of spectrum that would maximize its utility. The utility of the client can be modeled as

$$U_c = \alpha \, log \left(1 + \theta \, B \, log_2 \left(1 + \frac{p}{\sigma} \right) \right) - \gamma B \tag{4}$$

$$st. \ U_c \geq 0$$

$$B_{min} < B < B_{max}$$

where B_{min} and B_{max} represent minimum spectrum required to transmit the frame with uneven importance and the maximum spectrum available per user with the base station.

2.2   Utility of the Base Station (Service Provider)

Base station generates revenue by transmitting the multimedia data with QoE requirement to the client. The base station is rational and recognizes the client's QoE as a factor for the bandwidth requirement and spectrum cost. The payment received from the client ψ_{Client_SP} is modeled in Eq. (3). The base station also incurs two types of costs, namely the transmission cost and the spectrum cost. The utility equation for the base station can be modeled as:

$$U_{BS} = \psi_{Client\_SP} - \psi_{Tx} - \psi_{spectrum} \tag{5}$$

The transmission cost ψ_{Tx} is defined as the cost per unit energy required to transmit a frame over the wireless channel. It is determined by the packet length l, transmission power per bit p, constellation size of modulation scheme b and the spectrum B. λ is defined as the currency value per unit energy consumption.

$$\psi_{Tx} = \lambda \frac{lp}{bB} \tag{6}$$

The second cost incurred by the base station is the money paid to acquire the spectrum $\psi_{spectrum}$. The service provider might request the spectrum from the Federal Communications Commission (FCC) before it can use it for transmission of data. The cost function of the spectrum can be modeled as per [11] indicating that the cost mainly consists of investment φ which is directly proportional to B and a fixed cost μ. The cost co-efficient τ is non-negative constant and $\tau < 1$ for the cost function to be monotonically increasing and concave.

$$\psi_{spectrum} = \mu + \varphi(B)^\tau \tag{7}$$

The base station is interested in optimizing the cost it offers the client device for unit spectrum such that its net utility is maximized.

$$U_{BS} = \gamma B - \lambda \frac{lp}{bB} - \mu + \varphi(B)^{\tau} \tag{8}$$

$$st. \; U_{BS} \geq 0$$

$$\gamma \geq \lambda + \mu + \varphi$$

3   Stackelberg Game Analysis

The service provider and the client device, both being coherent, desire to maximize their profits by changing the cost of spectrum blocks and amount of spectrum requested, respectively. This utility maximizing problem is defined as a two stage Stackelberg game. In this section, we investigate the proposed Stackelberg game and compute the Nash equilibrium for the bandwidth allocation problem. Nash equilibrium of the game is defined as the set of strategies, one for client and one for the service provider such that both players have no incentive deviating from that strategy [12].

Since the client device always request the spectrum based on the cost charged by the base station, we define the service provider as the leader and client as the follower of the two stage Stackelberg game. We then use backward induction to solve the game. We begin with converting the utility function into best response functions and then we look for the mutual best response $\{B^*, \gamma^*\}$. Mutual best response is the set of strategies which produce the most favorable outcome for a player, taking other players' strategies as given [12]. The best response solution is generally attained by finding the Nash Equilibrium.

3.1   Best Response of the Client (End-User)

The service provider decides the cost for unit spectrum γ. The utility of the client is concave for any given cost γ and $B_{min} < B < B_{max}$ This can be proved computing the second derivative of the utility function.

$$\frac{\partial U_c}{\partial B} = \frac{\alpha \theta \log \left(1 + \frac{p}{\sigma}\right)}{B \theta \log \left(1 + \frac{p}{\sigma}\right) + 1} - \gamma \tag{9}$$

$$\frac{\partial^2 U_c}{\partial B^2} = -\frac{\alpha \theta^2 \log^2 \left(1 + \frac{p}{\sigma}\right)}{\left(B \theta \log \left(1 + \frac{p}{\sigma}\right) + 1\right)^2} \tag{10}$$

In the above equations, signal power, noise power, spectrum B and the payoff parameter α are all positive and so the second derivative $\partial^2 U_c / \partial B^2 < 0$. This proves that the utility function is concave for all cost values. The best response B^* or stable value of the function that would maximize the utility of the client can be computed by equating the first derivative to zero.

$$\frac{\alpha \theta \log \left(1 + \frac{p}{\sigma}\right)}{B \theta \log \left(1 + \frac{p}{\sigma}\right) + 1} - \gamma = 0 \tag{11}$$

By solving the Eq. (11), we determine the best response for the client. Equation (12) demonstrates that the users' spectrum requirement has the following relationship with the cost parameter γ.

$$B(\gamma) = \frac{\alpha\,\theta\,log\left(1 + \frac{p}{\sigma}\right) - \gamma}{\gamma\,\theta\,log\left(1 + \frac{p}{\sigma}\right)} \tag{12}$$

3.2   Best Response of the Base Station (Service Provider)

The service provider being the leader and a rational player of the game knows the best response of the client shown in Eq. (12) for any given cost γ. Therefore, the utility equation of the base station shown in Eq. (8) can be rewritten in terms of γ as

$$U_{BS} = \gamma\,B(\gamma) - \lambda\,\frac{lp}{bB(\gamma)} - \mu + \varphi(B(\gamma))^\tau \tag{13}$$

Obtaining the best response for the above utility equation is not straightforward and require numerical methods. Here, we have used couple of lemmas to prove that a Nash equilibrium exists and then use Newton's method to compute the best response.

Lemma 1. *A real function which is differentiable must be a continuous function, [13].*

Lemma 2. *A continuous real function on a closed interval must contain a maximum value and a minimum value, [13].*

Computing the first derivative of U_{BS} and $B(\gamma)$ with respect to γ, we obtain Eqs. (14) and (15). Therefore, it can be seen that the utility equation is both real and differentiable. By coupling with Lemma 1, we can prove that the utility function is continuous.

$$\frac{\partial U_{BS}(\gamma)}{\partial \gamma} = B(\gamma) + [B(\gamma) + \frac{lp}{bB(\gamma)} - \varphi\tau B(\gamma)^{\tau-1}]\frac{\partial B(\gamma)}{\partial \gamma} \tag{14}$$

$$\frac{\partial B(\gamma)}{\partial \gamma} = -\frac{\alpha}{\gamma^2} \tag{15}$$

Equation (9) can have more than one root, however we choose only the root which yields the maximum utility. Equation (12) illustrates the fixed relationship between the client's bandwidth requirement and the spectrum cost. Expression in (15) is always negative, this proves that the function B(γ) is monotonically decreasing. Therefore, it can be observed that the client would choose to request the maximum bandwidth when the spectrum cost is minimum and vice versa. The optimal value of the utility function is bounded by a closed interval $[\gamma_{min}, \gamma_{max}]$. The maximum and minimum cost of the spectrum can be derived from Eq. (12) and are defined in the equations below.

$$\gamma_{min} = \frac{\alpha\,\theta\,log\left(1 + \frac{p}{\sigma}\right)}{B_{max}\,\theta\,log\left(1 + \frac{p}{\sigma}\right) + 1} \tag{16}$$

$$\gamma_{max} = \frac{\alpha \, \theta \, log \left(1 + \frac{p}{\sigma}\right)}{B_{min} \, \theta \, log \left(1 + \frac{p}{\sigma}\right) + 1} \tag{17}$$

Combining Lemmas 1 and 2, we can prove the existence of a maximum value for U_{BS} within the closed interval $[\gamma_{min}, \gamma_{max}]$. The optimal cost response γ^* can be evaluated by finding the maximum value for U_{BS} using a genetic algorithm or global searching.

3.3   Stackelburg Equilibrium Algorithm

The mutual best response $\{B^*, \gamma^*\}$ is the Nash equilibrium of the Stackelberg game which maximizes the utility for both the service provider and client $\{U_{BS}, U_C\}$. Based on the above analysis of two-stage Stackelberg game we present an algorithm to determine the Nash Equilibrium using backward induction method. The Stackelberg game interactions are performed every time before a multimedia packet is transmitted.

The computing cost of the proposed algorithm is O (M), which comprises of the maximum iteration steps M to determine the optimal value. Alternatively, a searching table can be created and updated with the equilibrium spectrum and equilibrium cost during the sparse time periods between the multimedia transmission. The best responses can directly be searched from the table whenever the algorithm needs to be performed. This would reduce the computing complexity and latency in-between the data transmission. The global searching algorithm to compute the mutual best responses is shown below.

Algorithm 1: Computation of Stackelberg Game Equilibrium.

```
1.   Initialization:
     1.1 Initialize the cost parameters α, μ, λ, φ and τ.
     1.2 Define the channel parameters: transmission
         power p and channel noise σ.
     1.3 Set the transmission parameters: length of
         packet l and modulation constellation size b.
2.  Iterations:
     2.1 The algorithms solve for the best responses
         {B*,γ*}. Thereby, determining the utilities of
         the base station and the client {U_BS,U_C}.
     2.2 Set  U_BS = U_C = B* = γ* = 0.
     2.3 Let  χ = γ_min : N : γ_max
     2.4 For i=1: N
     2.5 Set  γ = χ(i)
     2.6 compute U_BS = γ B(γ) - λ (lp)/(bB(γ)) - μ + φ(B(γ))^τ
     2.7 If U_BS(γ) > U_BS
             2.7.1 Update  U_BS = U_BS(γ)
             2.7.2 Set  γ* = γ
             2.7.3 Calculate  B* = α log(1 + p/σ) - γ*/γ* (1 + p/σ)
```

2.7.4 Determine the value of U_C

3. Output:

The algorithm searches the closed interval space $[\gamma_{min}, \gamma_{max}]$ to determine the Stackelberg game equilibrium $\{B^*, \gamma^*\}$ and the corresponding utilities of base station and client $\{U_{BS}, U_C\}$

4 Simulations

The performance of the proposed game theoretic scheme has been examined in this section. The cost parameters are set as follows: $\alpha = 100$, $\mu = 10$, $\lambda = 1$, $\varphi = 1$ and $\tau = 0.5$. The channel SNR is set to 25 dB. The modulation size and length of packet are set at 2 and 10000, respectively. The network utilization θ is set at 50%. The Stackelberg game equilibrium for optimization for the service provider is facilitated by a global search. The utility of the base station is computed for payoff parameter $\alpha = 100$, 90 and 80 and the corresponding best responses (γ^*) is shown in Fig. 3.

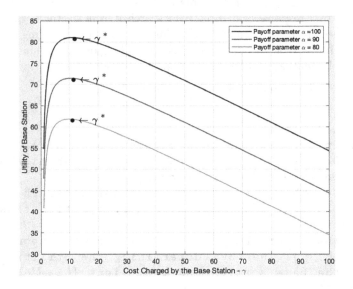

Fig. 3. Utility of base station versus cost

In Sect. 3, we showed mathematically, the existence of an equilibrium in the proposed Stackelberg game. The utility of the client primarily depends upon the channel conditions and the network utilization given by θ. The utility of the base station depends upon the amount of spectrum blocks allocated and the length of the packet l.

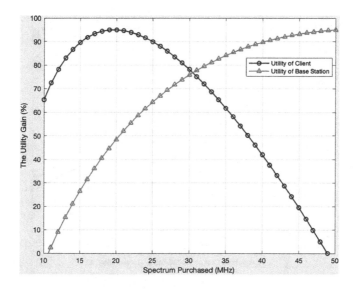

Fig. 4. Utility curves of base station and client device versus spectrum allocated

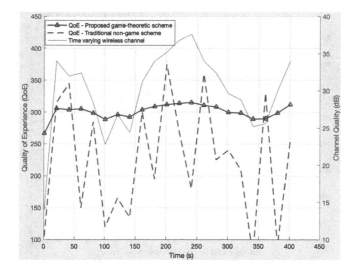

Fig. 5. Comparison of QoE versus time varying wireless channel

Figure 4 shows the utility gain of the base station and the client device for fixed cost (γ^*) versus different quantity of spectrum blocks allocated to the client. It can be observed that the utility of the base station increases linearly whereas the utility of the client is concave by its nature for any given cost γ. This graphically proves the existence of the Nash equilibrium.

The QoE of the end-user for the traditional non-game scheme is compared with the proposed game-theoretic scheme in the following simulations.

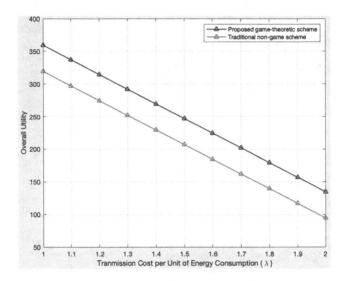

Fig. 6. Comparison of utility versus transmission cost per unit energy consumption

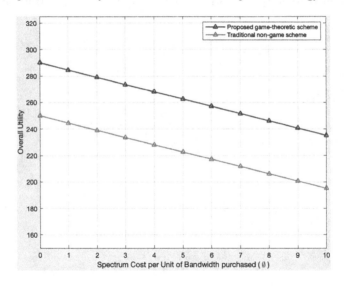

Fig. 7. Comparison of utility versus spectrum cost per unit bandwidth allocation

The quality of wireless channel is inherently time varying. In traditional methods, the client's QoE changes as a function of channel quality. However, in the proposed method, we use cost as a factor in the utility equation which improves the overall QoE of the user. In Fig. 5, the proposed game is performed each time before the multimedia packet is transmitted over the time varying channel. It can be observed that the QoE of the client is not compromised based on the channel quality.

The overall utility is defined as the sum of utilities of the SP and the end user. Figures 6 and 7 show the overall utility gain versus transmission cost per unit of energy consumption λ and the spectrum cost per unit of bandwidth allocated φ respectively. It can be observed that the overall utilities of both schemes vary with the cost parameters linearly. Thus, the different initializations of the cost parameters do not affect the proposed game theoretic scheme and they yield a better utility.

5   Conclusion

In this paper, we introduced the concept of game theoretic spectrum allocation by leveraging cost factor to determine the QoE in wireless multimedia communication. The proposed game was developed between the service provider with multiple, time-aligned versions of media files and a client device which requests video sequences. A two-stage Stackelberg game was set-up with service provider as the leader and client as the follower. The amount of spectrum allocation, and the cost of spectrum are the two variables in the game under which the Nash equilibrium was derived. Simulation results show that the QoE of the end user and the utility of the service provider improves significantly in comparison with the traditional non-game methods. The proposed game-theoretic methodology can be scaled to multiple user framework with a single service provider with multiple clients or multiple service providers with multiple clients.

Acknowledgement. This research was supported in part by National Science Foundation grants CNS-1743427 and CNS-1463768.

References

1. Baldemair, R., et al.: Evolving wireless communications: addressing the challenges and expectations of the future. IEEE Veh. Technol. Mag. **8**(1), 24–30 (2013)
2. Stockhammer, T.: Dynamic adaptive streaming over HTTP - standards and design principles. In: Proceedings of the 2nd Annual ACM Conference on Multimedia Systems, pp. 133–144 (2011)
3. MPEG: Information technology: Dynamic adaptive streaming over HTTP (DASH): Part 1: Media presentation description and segment formats. ISO/IEC 23009–1:2014 (2014)
4. Timmerer, C.: Advanced Transport Options for DASH: QUIC and HTTP/2 (2015). https://bitmovin.com/advanced-transport-options-dash-quic-http2/
5. He, S., Wang, W.: Context-aware QoE-price equilibrium for wireless multimedia relay communications using Stackelberg game. In: 2017 IEEE Conference on Computer Communications Workshops, pp. 506–511 (2017)
6. Wang, Q., Wang, W., Shi, J., Zhu, H., Zhang, N.: Smart media pricing (SMP): non-uniform packet pricing game for wireless multimedia communications. In: Proceedings of the IEEE International Conference on Computer Communications, the 5th Workshop on Smart Data Pricing, pp. 27–32 (2016)

7. Niyato, D., Hossain, E.: A game-theoretic approach to competitive spectrum sharing in cognitive radio networks. In: IEEE Wireless Communications and Networking Conference, pp. 16–20 (2007)

8. Huang, J., Wang, H.: Game user oriented multimedia transmission over cognitive radio networks. IEEE Trans. Circuits Syst. Video Technol. **27**(1), 108–208 (2017)

9. Yuan, H., Wei, X., Yang, F., Xiao, J., Kwong, S.: Cooperative bargaining game-based multiuser bandwidth allocation for dynamic adaptive streaming over HTTP. IEEE Trans. Multimedia **20**(1), 183–197 (2018)

10. Su, Z., Xu, Q., Fei, M., Dong, M.: Game theoretic resource allocation in media cloud with mobile social users. IEEE Trans. Multimedia **18**(8), 1650–1660 (2016)

11. Niyato, D., Hossain, E.: Competitive spectrum sharing in cognitive radio networks: a dynamic game approach. IEEE Trans. Wirel. Commun. **7**(7), 2651–2660 (2008)

12. Osborne, M.J.: An Introduction to Game Theory. Oxford University Press, Oxford (2003)

13. Binmore, K.G.: Mathematical Analysis: A Straightforward Approach. Cambridge University Press, Cambridge (1982)

14. Wang, W.: Collaborative multimedia source-protocol coordination: a cross-layer QoE study in modern wireless networks. IEEE Syst. J. **11**(4), 2403–2409 (2017)

15. Wang, W., Peng, D., Wang, H., Sharif, H., Chen, H.H.: Energy-constrained quality optimization for secure image transmission in wireless sensor networks. Adv. Multimedia **2007**, 1–9 (2007). Article ID 25187

Intrusion Detection at the Network Edge: Solutions, Limitations, and Future Directions

Simone Raponi$^{(\boxtimes)}$, Maurantonio Caprolu, and Roberto Di Pietro

College of Science and Engineering (CSE),
Division of Information and Computing Technology (ICT),
Hamad Bin Khalifa University (HBKU), Doha, Qatar
{sraponi,mcaprolu}@mail.hbku.edu.qa, rdipetro@hbku.edu.qa

Abstract. The low-latency, high bandwidth capabilities promised by 5G, together with the diffusion of applications that require high computing power and, again, low latency (such as videogames), are probably the main reasons—though not the only one—that have led to the introduction of a new network architecture: Fog Computing, that consists in moving the computation services geographically close to where computing is needed. This architectural shift moves security and privacy issues from the Cloud to the different layers of the Fog architecture. In this scenario, IDSs are still necessary, but they need to be contextualized in the new architecture. Indeed, while on the one hand Fog computing provides intrinsic benefits (e.g., low latency), on the other hand, it introduces new design challenges.

In this paper, we provide the following contributions: we analyze the possible IDS solutions that can be adopted within the different Fog computing tiers, together with their related deployment and design challenges; and, we propose some promising future directions, by taking into account the challenges left uncovered by the considered solutions.

1 Introduction

The data deluge expected by the massive adoption of IoT solutions, together with the need for better network performance required by modern end-user applications, underline how the classic network Cloud model is not able to efficiently respond to the new needs. The Cloud model offers a scalable infrastructure that frees users from the costs of designing, purchasing, and maintaining computing and storage resources. Despite the obvious advantages, this model is not suitable for latency sensitive applications, that demand geographical proximity with the service provider to meet their delay requirements. To address this challenge, Cisco researchers defined a new network architecture, called Fog Computing [1], that extends the Cloud computing paradigm to the edge of the network, enabling a new variety of applications and services, such as gaming, augmented reality, and real-time video stream processing. This new paradigm provides computational

T. Zhang et al. (Eds.): EDGE 2019, LNCS 11520, pp. 59–75, 2019.
https://doi.org/10.1007/978-3-030-23374-7_5

and storage capabilities physically closer to end-users, where data are being generated [2]. Among the characteristics of Fog Computing, the most important are [1]: low latency and location awareness; handling of a huge number of nodes; heterogeneity; widespread geographical distribution; support for mobile end-devices; support for real-time applications; and wireless access.

Since the Fog computing network architecture brings the typical services offered by Cloud computing closer to the end-user, most of its security and privacy issues are inherited from the Cloud itself. These problems include, but are not limited to, Distributed Denial of Service (DDoS) attacks, Man in the Middle (MitM) attacks, rogue gateway attacks, privacy leakage, privilege escalation attacks, service manipulation attacks, and injection of information. However, although the problems are the same in Fog computing, they should be contextualized in the new physical and logical elements of the Fog computing network architecture [3].

One of the most effective methods to solve the above-cited problems is the adoption of an Intrusion Detection System (IDS) to monitor and analyze the network traffic and the devices' behavior. Nevertheless, even IDSs need to be contextualized to the new network architecture. Indeed, designing an effective IDS requires to choose not only the IDS typology (e.g., Host-based IDS, Network-based IDS) and the methods of detection (e.g., anomaly-based IDS, signature-based IDS), but also the tier in the Fog computing architecture where to place it. Since the Fog computing network architecture is composed of three tiers, the placement of an IDS within a tier with respect to the others would completely change its capabilities.

Although the implementation of IDSs within the Fog Computing network architecture poses many challenges, whether inherited from the Cloud architecture or not, the introduced benefits could make the difference in certain scenario (e.g., the detection time plays a crucial role in defending a critical infrastructure).

Contributions: In this paper, we first provide an in-depth analysis of the IDSs implementation within the Fog computing network architecture by both identifying several design and deployment challenges inherited by the Cloud environment, and proposing new original ones. Further, we provide a detailed overview of a selected set of existing solutions. Among the proposed IDS solutions in the literature we considered both the ones specifically implemented for the Fog computing network architecture and the generic ones that have not been thought for the Fog paradigm—though they could be adopted within one or more Fog tiers (e.g., IDS for IoT devices that could be deployed in edge devices, IDS for Cloud). Moreover, we have mapped each existing solution to the challenges identified during the analysis, highlighting how none of the current solutions is able to satisfy most of them. Finally, we propose some future directions, taking into consideration the challenges left uncovered by the analyzed solutions.

Road-Map: The paper is organized as follows. In Sect. 2, we provide a technical background of the Fog computing network architecture. In Sect. 3, we study advantages and drawbacks that possible implementations of IDS in the Fog computing network architecture would bring. In Sect. 4, we provide an analysis of the main challenges related to architectural design and deployment of IDS in the Fog computing network architecture. The description of the existing solutions is performed in Sect. 5, together with the related mapping to the challenges previously identified. In Sect. 6, we discuss the results and propose some future directions, while in Sect. 7 we report some concluding remarks.

2   Background

In this section, an overview of both Edge and Fog Computing is provided, together with their differences.

Although apparently similar and often interchangeably used, Edge Computing and Fog Computing present key differences that are not always easy to catch. Both the network architectures share the same main objective: bringing the computation closer to the user, thus reducing the network congestion and the end-to-end delay. As highlighted in [4], the differences concern:

1. *how data are handled.* How to process and analyze data gathered locally or received by other devices in the network;
2. *where to process data.* Where to put both intelligence and computing power. The common architecture is composed of several tiers, the choice of the intelligence and computing power placement is crucial and strongly dependent on the purpose.

In Edge Computing, each end-device plays an important active role in processing data locally rather than delegate it to the Cloud [4]. As a consequence, every device, being it a sensor, an actuator, or a network device, relies on its own computational power and storage resources to perform operations on data. The product of this analysis could be maintained locally in case the device is autonomous and able to take advantage of this information, otherwise, it is delivered to other upper-tiers devices, that are usually responsible for both the management of the device itself and other devices belonging to the same subnetwork. On the contrary, in Fog Computing, processing power and storage resources needed to process and analyze data collected from IoT devices are integrated into other devices that, in turn, are moved geographically closer to the data collection. Usually, the devices in question are network ones, placed only a few hops away from the edge devices [5].

2.1   Fog Computing

Figure 1 depicts one of the most widely adopted architectures in Fog Computing: the Three-Tier Fog computing architecture [4].

Tier 1 – Edge Devices. Tier 1 usually consists of Internet of Things devices, including sensors (e.g., temperature, proximity, pressure, chemical, motion detection, optical), actuators (e.g., chemical, power generation, pumps, valves), and

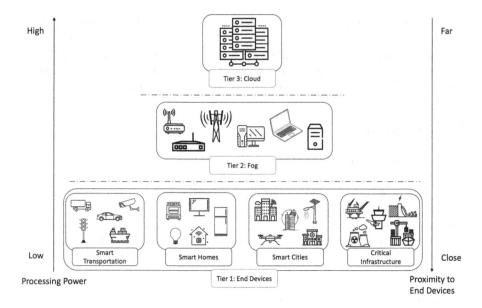

Fig. 1. Fog computing tiers

smart hand-held devices (e.g., smartphones, tablets, smart watches). Being the farthest from the Cloud tier, tier 1 includes devices that directly interact both with end-users and the surrounding environment, gathering data and information that need to be processed. However, most of these devices suffer from limited memory and limited computational power, thus being unable to apply algorithms for the analysis and the processing of the data in a limited time [6]. This limitation leads to the need to move the computation to more suitable places: in the Cloud, or within the tier 2 in case Fog computing network architectures have been adopted.

Tier 2 – Fog Devices. Tier 2 represents the layer between the end-user devices and the Cloud. It usually consists of network devices (including switches, routers, gateways), WAN/MAN (Wide Area Network/Metropolitan Area Network) access devices, multiplexers, Integrated Access Devices, and requires considerable resource requirements to perform several tasks, including real-time data processing and analysis, data storing, data caching, and computational offloading [7]. In this layer, the analysis performed on the gathered data obtained from the edge devices allows to take decisions locally, thus providing quick responses to unusual behaviors [8].

Tier 3 – Cloud. Tier 3 comprises the traditional Cloud servers. Cloud servers, for savings and efficiency reasons, are kept in dedicated facilities (i.e., data centers) that, in turn, are placed in convenient geographical locations (e.g., where electricity is cheaper and the weather conditions are optimal). This leads to an unavoidable physical distance between the Cloud server and end-users, that eventually brings to end-to-end communication delays and network congestion. However, Cloud servers offer more computing power and more data storage with respect to devices in tier 2, together with the opportunity to perform computationally burdensome operations, such as management of big data and parallel data processing.

3   Intrusion Detection at the Network Edge

As a new in-standardization-phase network architecture, Fog Computing presents several security and privacy challenges. Indeed, although the Cloud architecture is commonly protected by Cloud operators, security and privacy solutions are not effortlessly extensible for the new architectures introduced. Challenges of these architectures include, but are not limited to, malicious insider attacks detection, malicious node detection, Fog forensics, intra-tier and inter-tier secure communication (i.e., authentication and integrity of the data exchanged), trust in the Fog services, trust in the end-users, cross-border privacy of data, security in the storage of the data, security and privacy in the computation of the data, and access control policies [4,9]. Since the Fog computing network architecture is continuously evolving, these challenges have only been partially addressed in the literature.

This section focuses on the detection of malicious attacks performed by internal/external attackers, by describing the possible implementations of IDSs in both the Cloud architecture and the Fog Computing network architecture. Attacks can come both from inside and outside the network. We consider:

- *outside attack*: any attack coming from outside the network or performed by a non-authenticated device;
- *inside attack*: any attack coming from inside the network and performed by an authenticated device.

Inside attacks are more difficult to detect, especially in multi-tenant environments where resources are shared among different applications and users. Moreover, attackers from the inside could use their knowledge of the system to cover their tracks, thus remaining transparent.

The Fog computing network architecture presents some peculiarities with respect to the Cloud architecture that could make an IDS more suitable and effective. The Fog computing network architecture is composed of three tiers, each tier offering a different view of the network: the higher the tier, the wider the vision on the network; conversely, the lower the tier, the narrower the vision on the network.

Advantages and drawbacks of implementing an IDS in the Fog computing network architecture with respect to the Cloud computing network architecture are depicted in Table 1. Each row in the table represents where it could be possible to deploy an IDS, while in each column a Fog computing feature is reported.

Table 1. Features of IDSs implemented in different network architectures.

		Comp. power	Storage	Bandwidth	Latency	Network view	Privacy threat
Cloud		High	High	High	High	High	High
Fog	Tier 3	High	High	High	High	High	High
	Tier 2	Medium	Medium	Medium	Low	Medium	Medium
	Tier 1	Low	Low	N/A	N/A	Low	Low

3.1   Implementing an IDS in the Cloud Servers

Implementing an IDS in the Cloud Servers or, equivalently, in Tier 3 of the Fog computing network architecture, allows to exploit the powerful resources of the Cloud devices, thus providing the IDS with remarkable *Computational Power* and *Storage* resources. Furthermore, the physical characteristics of the Cloud allow application and services to rely on an efficient and performing network, which guarantees an outstanding *Bandwidth*. However, the modern needs for a smart and connected world lead to a massive generation of data from edge devices spread all over the world. Considering that Cloud Servers are usually physically far from the edge devices, implementing an IDS on a Cloud Server implies high *latency* and delay times, inescapably dictated by the physical distance between the communicating devices. Being virtually placed at the highest point of the network, Cloud Servers have a far-reaching *Network View*, made available by devices located in lower levels that share information regarding their local view of the network. This gives an IDS the possibility to manage threats having a complete picture of the network available. Finally, an IDS has the ability to monitor data traffic and scan files in order to detect malicious code and unusual behaviors. Cloud service providers, to make the most of the computational and storage resources they own, rely on multi-tenant environments where users share the same machine, often without being aware of it. Although this approach is extremely cost-effective from the resources optimization's point of view, it opens the door to potentially serious privacy issues. In fact, regardless of the technology used (e.g., virtual machines, containers), there is an impressive amount of attacks aimed at undermining security and privacy of information on the Cloud [10].

3.2   Implementing an IDS in the Fog Network Architecture

The Fog computing network architecture, as depicted in Fig. 1, consists of three tiers, where each tier is composed of a specific set of devices: tier 1 includes edge devices, representing those devices that allow generating data, such as sensors, actuators, and smart-hand devices; tier 2 includes Fog devices, that are usually placed geographically close to the edge devices and perform processing and analysis services; tier 3 represents the Cloud itself. The advantages and drawbacks of an IDS in the Fog computing network architecture are strongly dependent on the tier in which it is implemented.

Implementing an IDS within the tier 3 makes no difference compared to implementing it within the Cloud since Fog computing network architecture's tier 3 and Cloud coincide. Conversely, the implementation of an IDS within the tier 2 presents some differences. Tier 2's devices, often represented by network devices (i.e., switches, routers, gateways), small servers, Integrated Access Devices, can boast of adequate *computational power* and *storage* resources, not even remotely comparable to those in the Cloud but sufficient to successfully perform data mining, data aggregation, and data processing tasks. Implementing an IDS within an existing network device would reduce the cost of acquisition, commissioning, and maintenance of a new device, with the disadvantage of subtracting computational resources from an operating network device. Furthermore, tier's 2 network devices could be not able to perform Intrusion Detection activities and manage the incoming traffic peaks in parallel, thus incurring in bottlenecks that could reduce the response time, and so the usefulness, of the IDS. The IDS can even be implemented within edge devices, placed at tier 1. In this latter case, considering that devices have poor *computational power* and *storage* resources, only lightweight IDSs (e.g., [11–13]) can be taken into account. Moreover, the Cloud's tier makes use of dedicated network backbones designed to handle a worldwide traffic volume, while tier 2's devices can only offer a limited *bandwidth*, having been designed to handle local traffic volumes. The bandwidth metrics do not make sense if we consider a tier 1's IDS, given that it would be directly integrated within the end-device. The *latency* is the metric that motivates the need to have IDSs within tier 2's devices. In fact, the geographic distance between Cloud servers and edge devices generating the data increases the *latency* in a perceptible way, an increase that could be critical in certain contexts (e.g., in a critical infrastructure scenario taking timely decisions is crucial, not respecting the right timing could lead to catastrophic events). The *Network View* becomes wider and wider with the increase of the tier, that is with the increase of the geographical distance from the edge devices. In fact, an IDS implemented within a tier 1's edge device enjoys only a limited vision of the network, that is the vision of the component itself (or of a small subset of them). Turning to tier 2, the devices receive data from subnetworks composed of edge devices, thus having the ability to both correlate and aggregate information, obtaining a wider vision of the network. Tier 3 exploits the information of tier 2's devices usually located in geographically distant places, that provide it with a peripheral view of the whole network. On the contrary, moving towards higher tiers, the threats related to the *privacy* of data and information tend to increase. In fact, considering that optimizing the use of resources leads to a maximization of the gain, the devices tend to serve as many clients as possible (and to manage as many devices of the lower tier as possible). The more information (often also important and sensitive) a device contains, the more this device is tempting for an attacker who, be it internal or external, will have at her disposal various means to appropriate or compromise information. For example, a malicious employee could inject malware into a competitor company's network and mask the traces, compromising the information of a device that is dealing with the detection.

4   Challenges

In this section, we provide an in-depth analysis of the main challenges related to the architectural design and deployment of an IDS within the Fog. The new architecture introduced by the Fog computing network paradigm brings the typical services offered by Cloud computing closer to the end-user. For this reason, most of the security and privacy issues of the Fog computing architecture are inherited from the Cloud. Similar considerations can be applied to IDSs deployed within a Fog computing network architecture, that mainly have the same IDSs challenges as Cloud environments, in addition to new ones derived from IoT environments. We discuss all these challenges in the following subsections, starting from some considerations on the deployment of IDSs in the Fog computing network architecture environment that lead to some generally valid challenges, regardless of the type of IDS and the layer of the Fog computing network architecture in which it is deployed. Then, we present other challenges that arise depending on the type of IDS considered (Table 2).

4.1   Deployment

One of the first architectural problem to be considered before designing an IDS for the Fog computing network architecture environment is to define in which of the three tiers the single components of the system should be deployed. IDSs can be deployed within the tier 1 to detect malicious behavior by monitoring and analyzing log files, user login information, and enforcing access control policies. IDSs can also be deployed within the tier 2 to detect malicious attacks such as Denial of Service (DoS), port scanning, to name a few [9]. In order to increase the security level of the entire network, IDSs must be deployed in all the three tiers, monitoring and analyzing traffic and behavior of edge devices, Fog devices, and Cloud servers. In fact, securing one or two tiers of the Fog computing network architecture is not sufficient to protect the entire system, dangerous events like the propagation of malware from a compromised device to the rest of the network could not be noticed [4]. The deployment of IDS solutions within every tier of the Fog computing network architecture leads to common challenges, described in Sect. 4.2, as well as to specific ones depending on the type of IDS considered, discussed in Sect. 4.3.

4.2   General Challenges

Considering the Fog computing network architecture peculiarities described in Sect. 3, implementing a reliable and efficient IDS implies designing and tuning a detection system able to effectively work in an environment with the following characteristics:

- **Large-scale Network:** The large number of heterogeneous connected devices, as well as the unpredictable chaotic dynamics of today's large and medium-size computer networks, make the number of suspicious events that need to be controlled by an IDS huge. For this reason, IDSs should both be equipped with hardware resources adequate to support this workload and implement powerful algorithms to efficiently perform the required tasks.
- **Geo-distributed Environment:** In sharp contrast with the more centralized Cloud, the Fog could be very complex and geographically worldwide distributed, depending on the purpose for which it was designed [1]. As an example, we can consider a wireless sensor network deployed along a highway that crosses an entire country, providing lighting and video surveillance services. In this case, edge devices could be deployed every 100 m, while Fog devices could be deployed every kilometer. All these devices could send data to a Cloud located halfway around the world. In this scenario, an IDS should be able to provide a real-time protection to the entire architecture.
- **Real-time Notification:** The most important characteristic of every IDS is the ability to early discover intrusion violation threats. The huge number of connected edge devices, as well as their geographic distances (that have a severe impact on the network latency), make it difficult to analyze packets in real-time. This increases the notification time, impacting negatively on the response time.
- **Alarm Parallelization:** Securing all the Fog computing network architecture layers requires a distributed IDS system, with at least one component in every layer of the architecture. These components need to cooperate with each other by exchanging data that can be aggregated to obtain a comprehensive high-level view of the network, improving the overall reliability and reactiveness of the whole system.
- **False-alarm Control:** The main objective of an IDS is to raise alarm if an event in the network could be considered as an intrusion. The verification of whether a suspicious event is a real attack or a false positive is beyond the scope of current IDS solutions [14]. The Fog computing characteristics, discussed in Sect. 1, could increase the false positive/negative events detected by the system. For this reason, more efforts are needed to improve the IDSs detection accuracy.

Table 2. IDS design challenges

IDS type	Challenges
Host-Based Intrusion Detection System (Tier 1)	• Limited Resources (Comp. Power, Storage, Battery) • Lack of Context Knowledge • Delay in Centralized Reporting
Host-Based Intrusion Detection System (Tier 2)	• Lack of Context Knowledge • Delay in Centralized Reporting
Network-Based Intrusion Detection System (Tiers 1, 2, 3)	• Insider Attackers Detection • Cooperation • Decrease False Positives/Negatives • Encrypted Traffic • Developing Physical Jamming Detection Techniques • Developing DoS Detection and Mitigation Techniques
General	• Large-Scaling • Geo-Distribution • Environment Dynamicity • Real-time Notification • Alarm Parallelization • False-alarm Control

4.3 Design

The design challenges are different depending on the type of IDS considered (*Host-based* or *Network-based*) and the tier in which it is intended to be placed. The main challenges of deploying *host-based* IDS in the Fog computing network architecture are aligned with the ones of other network architectures:

– **Lack of Context Knowledge:** Having only its local view, a host-based IDS is not aware of what is happening outside. This lack of context knowledge makes more challenging to achieve high detection accuracy.
– **Delay in Centralized Reporting:** As part of a more complex system charged with supervising the whole Fog computing network, a host-based IDS has to report every detected local anomaly to a centralized entity. This entity is charged with the collection and elaboration of the data coming from every other component in the network. If the communication between this centralized module and the other components of the system has high latency due to their geographical distribution, the delay in centralizing reporting becomes very challenging, impacting the overall performance and accuracy of the IDS.

If the IDS is deployed within the tier 1, another challenge arises:

– **Limited Resources:** Since edge devices usually have very limited resources (i.e., in terms of computation, network bandwidth, storage, and battery), designing and implementing IDSs within the tier 1 could be very challenging.

For *network-based* IDSs instead, the main challenges are applicable to each tier of the Fog computing network architecture:

- **Insider Attackers Detection:** The attacks coming from inside the network are usually very challenging to discover. In fact, edge devices with genuine authentication privileges are often able to cover their traces and hide evidence of their malicious activities.
- **Cooperation:** If the IDS solution includes different modules, regardless of the tasks they are performing, they still need to cooperate with each other, adding further typical distributed systems' challenges.
- **Decrease False Positives/Negatives:** In the context of IDS, a high number of false positives makes the solution unusable due to the waste of resources dedicated to analyzing legitimate events. Moreover, false negatives make the solution ineffective, because malicious events would go unnoticed.
- **Encrypted Traffic:** A network-based IDS, due to its physical position, is able to observe the entire network traffic generated by the subnet it is connected to. However, if the traffic is encrypted, it is not able to open the packets and analyze their content. This limitation makes the detection of malicious packets more challenging.
- **Developing DoS Detection and Mitigation Techniques:** The Fog computing network architecture moves services from the Cloud to local Fog devices which, having less network bandwidth and being less protected, are more vulnerable to DoS attacks.

If the IDS is a Wireless IDS (WIDS), also the following challenge arises:

- **Developing Physical Jamming Detection Techniques:** Tier 1 is mostly composed of IoT sensor networks, which normally communicate both with each other and with Fog devices via wireless networks. This makes them vulnerable to physical level's DoS attacks, such as jamming attacks.

5   Existing Solutions

In this section we provide a thorough analysis of the studies related to IDSs present in the literature.

Given the widespread adoption of the Fog computing network architecture, in recent years several studies have come to light, with the aim of proposing solutions for the integration of efficient IDSs within the new paradigm. In [8], the authors introduced a lightweight IDS based on an Artificial Immune System (AIS), that is a form of biologically inspired computing. The AIS takes inspiration from the Human Immune System (HIS), that protects the body against the diseases being able to recognize external pathogens among internal cells and molecules of the body. The proposed IDS is developed in all the three tiers of the Fog computing network architecture. In tier 1, detectors are deployed within the edge devices. In tier 2, devices take advantage of a smart data concept to analyze and process the intrusion alerts. Smart data is a smart structure that helps to manage a large amount of data in IoT applications: a simple lightweight data cell that evolves (by merging with other cells or dividing by them, according to the direction) when traveling across the tiers. Finally, in tier 3 the IDS organizes the network traffic in clusters (by relying on unsupervised clustering techniques) and trains the detectors.

In [15] the authors found in the Device security, thus in the identification of malicious edge devices, one of the major challenges for successfully integrate Fog Computing and Internet of Things. Taking into account the difficulty of preventing attacks from malicious Fog devices, due to their privileges of storing and processing data, the authors proposed a framework that makes use of three distinctive technologies: a two-stage Markov Model, an IDS, and a Virtual Honeypot Device (VHD). The two-stage Markov Model allows reducing the false alarm rate generated by the different types of data sent by the IoT devices. In detail, when the anomaly-based IDS detects a malicious behavior on the Fog device an attack alarm is generated and sent to the two-stage Markov Model. The first stage allows categorizing the Fog devices, while the second stage is dedicated to predicting whether the categorized devices have to be moved to the VHD or not. The VHD allows to store and maintain a log repository of all the identified malicious Fog devices and provides the system with protection against unknown attacks.

Furthermore, considering that the Fog computing network architecture provides the sensors networks with ever-increasing importance, several studies have introduced proposals of IDSs implementation within the aforementioned resource-constrained devices. In [16], the authors introduced a lightweight IDS based on a vector space representation using a single hidden layer MultiLayer Perceptron (MLP) to improve the detection time. The authors exploited new datasets, the Australian Defense Force Academy Linux Dataset (ADFA-LD) and the Australian Defense Force Academy Windows Dataset (ADFA-WD), respectively, representing system calls datasets containing both attacks and exploits on various applications. The proposed IDS, implemented within a Raspberry Pi as a Fog device, achieves 94% accuracy, 95% recall, and 92% F1-measure in ADFA-LD, and 74% accuracy, 74% recall, and 74% F1-measure in ADFA-WD when considering a small number of nodes. Another IDS able to run within resource-constrained devices has been introduced in [17]. The authors reached a convenient trade-off between the energy consumption and the accuracy detection by making use of an anomaly-based IDS only when the signature of a new attack, identified by a signature-based IDS, is expected to occur. The problem is formulated as a security game model, where the security strategy is a game formulation between the intruder's attack and the IDS agent implemented within an Internet of Things device. The IDS agent implements its anomaly detection techniques to detect new attack patterns by relying on the Nash Equilibrium. The performance and the viability of the proposed approach have been analyzed by simulating a Wireless Sensor Network (WSN) using the TOSSIM simulator.

However, at the top of the new network architecture, the Cloud continues to be omnipresent, so more and more innovative studies have been proposed with the goal of implementing IDSs within the Cloud (or within the Fog computing network architecture's tier 3). In [18], the authors proposed an anomaly detection system at the hypervisor layer that makes use of Hybrid algorithms (e.g., Fuzzy C-Means clustering techniques, Artificial Neural Networks) to improve the accuracy of the detection system. The proposal has been experimented by using the DARPA's Knowledge Discovery and Data Mining (KDD) cup dataset, showing a higher detection accuracy and a lower false alarm rate even against low-frequent attacks, thus outperforming Naive Bayes classifiers and Classic ANN techniques.

In [19], the authors introduced a framework of Cooperative IDSs to counteract Distributed Denial of Service (DDoS) attacks on the Cloud. IDSs placed in the Cloud computing regions exchange alerts with each other. Each of them relies on a cooperative agent that is able to determine whether to accept the alert received from other IDSs or not. If the agent decides to accept the alert, the system adds a new blocking rule (related to the identification of the type of packet in the Cloud region) into the block table. A comparison against a pure Snort-based IDS shows that the proposed solution allows more accurate detection of Distributed Denial of Service attacks, paying only a small additional computational effort.

6 Discussion and Future Directions

Nowadays, several systems such as SCADA, Cloud, and Smart Grid rely on IDSs as the first line of defense against malicious attacks such as Scanning attacks, DoS attacks, Insider attacks, and Man in the Middle attacks [4]. For this reason, after the introduction of the Fog computing network architecture, a new line of research started studying the adoption of IDSs within this paradigm. Since the advantages of each IDS are strongly dependent on the tiers in which it is implemented, to increase the level of security, the IDSs should be deployed in every tier of the architecture. However, this choice brings new challenges, discussed in Sect. 4.

In this section, we first evaluate the mapping between existing solutions and these challenges, highlighting which challenges have not been addressed by the solutions in the literature, then we propose promising future directions.

Table 3 shows the mapping between the existing solutions in the literature and the challenges we identified during our analysis. A horizontal cut of the table allows to know whether the challenge has been addressed by the considered work, while a vertical cut provides an overview of the challenges addressed by single solutions. It is possible to notice how most of the solutions in the literature focused on solving the typical challenges of distributed systems (e.g., geographic distribution, large-scaling, environmental dynamicity, real-time notification, alarm parallelization, and delay in centralized reporting). This is justified by the fact that these solutions aim at leveraging the most important advantage offered by the Fog computing network architecture (i.e., the reduction of the network latency). This property allows Edge devices within the tier 1,

Table 3. Mapping between existing solutions and challenges *Legend: N/D: Not Declared, N/A: Not Applicable*

Challenges/Studies	[8]	[15]	[16]	[17]	[18]	[19]
Limited Resources	N/D	N/A	✗	✓	✗	✗
Lack of Context Knowledge	✓	✗	✗	✗	✓	✓
Delay in Centralized Reporting	✓	✓	✓	✗	✓	✓
Insider Attack Detection	✓	✗	✗	✓	✗	✗
Cooperation	✓	✗	✗	N/A	N/A	✓
Decrease False Positives/Negatives	✗	✓	✗	✓	✗	✓
Encrypted Traffic	✗	✗	N/A	N/A	✗	✗
Jamming Detection	✗	✗	✗	✗	N/A	N/A
DoS Detection	✓	✗	✗	✗	✓	✓
Large-Scaling	✓	✓	✓	N/A	✓	✓
Geographic Distribution	✓	✗	✓	N/A	✓	✓
Environment Dynamicity	✗	✓	✓	N/A	✓	✓
Real-time Notification	✓	✓	✓	✓	✓	✓
Alarm Parallelization	✓	✓	✓	N/A	N/A	✓
False-alarm Control	✗	✓	✗	✗	✗	✓

to quickly communicate with Fog devices within the tier 2, enabling more immediate aggregation and processing of data. In the context of IDS, this translates into improving the overall detection times of malicious events in the system.

However, most of the solutions did not focus on solving other important challenges, such as the development of lightweight IDSs able to work within resource-constrained devices, the false-alarm control, the reduction of false positive/negative number, and the DoS attack protection.

Tier 1 is typically composed of resource-constrained devices, with a limited amount of computational power, storage, and energy. These restrictions make the deployment of IDSs solutions within this tier challenging. In [17], for example, the authors proposed a lightweight detection technique that requires low energy consumption to achieve a high-security level.

Regarding the false-alarm control challenge, we believe that every IDS should have a validation mechanism for those events that are considered malicious, with the goal of decreasing the number of false positives. A possible solution requires to use more than one IDS's method of detection (i.e., signature-based, anomaly-based), that would also reduce the number of false negatives. In the context of IDSs, reducing false positives and false negatives is crucial, since a high number of false positives makes the solution unusable due to the waste of resources dedicated to analyzing legitimate events (that would be infeasible if the IDS has been deployed in a resource-constrained device), while false negatives make the solution ineffective, because malicious events would go unnoticed. Authors in [15] introduced a two-stage Markov module that helps to reduce the false-alarm rate of the IDSs.

The goal of some critical attacks on the Fog is to limit or deny the system services accessible to legitimate users/devices through Denial of Service attacks. In addition to the classic DoS attacks present in the literature, Edge devices could be infected by stealthy malware, that would consume their resources, finally leading to alternative DoS attacks. Although several solutions have been designed [20, 21], this research field is still worthy of attention, and further contributions are needed to effectively face this challenge.

Table 3 also highlights that the existing solutions we took into account do not adequately respond to the encrypted traffic challenge. This stems from the fact that most of the solutions designed to work in the presence of encrypted traffic are limited to the detection of some specific types of attacks, such as scanning, brute-force, and DoS attacks, and are ineffective for all the others [22]. Advanced machine and deep learning techniques, together with deep packet inspection methods, could be integrated within an IDS with the goal of analyzing encrypted traffic to detect malicious patterns.

Another important future direction regards the integration of some jamming detection techniques on IDSs deployed within both tier 1 and 2 of the Fog computing network architecture. This would allow to detect jamming attacks and to react by putting in place specific countermeasures. For example, if we take into account a wireless sensor network deployed within the tier 1 that communicates with a Fog gateway (placed within the tier 2), a malicious user could be able to completely block the inter-tiers communication by jamming the wireless channel. One possible detection approach, deployed within the tier 2, involves the monitoring of the packet's throughput. A drastic fall of this parameter for one or more Edge devices detected by a Fog device could be strong evidence of malicious jamming activities. The detection of this attack is crucial because techniques aimed at restoring the communication could be implemented, such as relying on alternatives schemes [23].

It is worth mentioning that most of the challenges identified in Sect. 4 could be addressed by using SDN networks technologies, as highlighted by [24], that investigated the possible cooperation between Edge computing and SDN. In this field, a promising research direction is the implementation of security mechanisms using SDN switches with stateful data plane [25] within the tier 2 of the Fog architecture.

7   Conclusions

In this paper, we analyzed how the changes in the network architecture introduced by the adoption of Fog Computing affect both the design and the deployment of IDSs. We first discussed the benefits of implementing an IDS within both the Cloud and the Fog network paradigm. Later, we identified the main challenges in the design and the deployment of IDS solutions within the Fog computing network architecture. Then, we explored a selected set of existing solutions and we mapped them to the challenges identified. Finally, we discussed the results and proposed some promising future research directions.

Acknowledgement. This publication was partially supported by awards NPRP-S-11-0109-180242, UREP23-065-1-014, and NPRP X-063-1-014 from the QNRF-Qatar National Research Fund, a member of The Qatar Foundation. The information and views set out in this publication are those of the authors and do not necessarily reflect the official opinion of the QNRF.

References

1. Bonomi, F., Milito, R., Zhu, J., Addepalli, S.: Fog computing and its role in the internet of things. In: Proceedings of the First Edition of the MCC Workshop on Mobile Cloud Computing, pp. 13–16. ACM (2012)
2. Rios, R., Roman, R., Onieva, J.A., Lopez, J.: From SMOG to Fog: a security perspective. In: 2017 Second International Conference on Fog and Mobile Edge Computing (FMEC), pp. 56–61, May 2017
3. Roman, R., Lopez, J., Mambo, M., Mobile edge computing, Fog et al.: A survey and analysis of security threats and challenges. Future Gener. Comput. Syst. **78**, 680–698 (2018)
4. Mukherjee, M., et al.: Security and privacy in fog computing: challenges. IEEE Access **5**, 19293–19304 (2017)
5. Munir, K.: Advancing Consumer-Centric Fog Computing Architectures. IGI Global (2018)
6. Sciancalepore, S., Piro, G., Vogli, E., Boggia, G., Grieco, L.A., Cavone, G.: LICITUS: a lightweight and standard compatible framework for securing layer-2 communications in the IoT. Comput. Netw. **108**, 66–77 (2016)
7. Yu, W., et al.: A survey on the edge computing for the internet of things. IEEE Access **6**, 6900–6919 (2018)
8. Hosseinpour, F., Vahdani Amoli, P., Plosila, J., Hämäläinen, T., Tenhunen, H.: An intrusion detection system for fog computing and IoT based logistic systems using a smart data approach. Int. J. Digit. Content Technol. Appl. **10**, 34–46 (2016)
9. Yi, S., Qin, Z., Li, Q.: Security and privacy issues of fog computing: a survey. In: Xu, K., Zhu, H. (eds.) WASA 2015. LNCS, vol. 9204, pp. 685–695. Springer, Cham (2015). https://doi.org/10.1007/978-3-319-21837-3_67
10. Martin, A., Raponi, S., Combe, T., Di Pietro, R.: Docker ecosystem-vulnerability analysis. Comput. Commun. **122**, 30–43 (2018)
11. Krontiris, I., Giannetsos, T., Dimitriou, T.: LIDeA: a distributed lightweight intrusion detection architecture for sensor networks. In: Proceedings of the 4th International Conference on Security and Privacy in Communication Networks, p. 20. ACM (2008)
12. Hai, T.H., Huh, E.N., Jo, M.: A lightweight intrusion detection framework for wireless sensor networks. Wirel. Commun. Mob. Comput. **10**(4), 559–572 (2010)
13. Onat, I., Miri, A.: An intrusion detection system for wireless sensor networks. In: IEEE International Conference on Wireless and Mobile Computing, Networking And Communications, WiMob 2005, vol. 3, pp. 253–259. IEEE (2005)
14. Anwar, S., et al.: From intrusion detection to an intrusion response system: fundamentals, requirements, and future directions. Algorithms **10**(2), 39 (2017)
15. Sandhu, R., Sohal, A.S., Sood, S.K.: Identification of malicious edge devices in fog computing environments. Inf. Secur. J.: Glob. Perspect. **26**(5), 213–228 (2017)
16. Sudqi Khater, B., Abdul Wahab, A., Idris, M., Abdulla Hussain, M., Ahmed Ibrahim, A.: A lightweight perceptron-based intrusion detection system for fog computing. Appl. Sci. **9**(1), 178 (2019)

17. Sedjelmaci, H., Senouci, S.M., Al-Bahri, M.: A lightweight anomaly detection technique for low-resource IoT devices: a game-theoretic methodology. In: 2016 IEEE International Conference on Communications (ICC), pp. 1–6. IEEE (2016)
18. Pandeeswari, N., Kumar, G.: Anomaly detection system in cloud environment using fuzzy clustering based ANN. Mob. Netw. Appl. **21**(3), 494–505 (2016)
19. Lo, C.C., Huang, C.C., Ku, J.: A cooperative intrusion detection system framework for cloud computing networks. In: 2010 39th International Conference on Parallel Processing Workshops, pp. 280–284. IEEE (2010)
20. Di Pietro, R., Mancini, L.V.: Intrusion detection systems, vol. 38. Springer, Heidelberg (2008). https://doi.org/10.1007/978-0-387-77265-3
21. Abeshu, A., Chilamkurti, N.: Deep learning: the frontier for distributed attack detection in fog-to-things computing. IEEE Commun. Mag. **56**(2), 169–175 (2018)
22. Kovanen, T., David, G., Hämäläinen, T.: Survey: intrusion detection systems in encrypted traffic. In: Galinina, O., Balandin, S., Koucheryavy, Y. (eds.) NEW2AN/ruSMART -2016. LNCS, vol. 9870, pp. 281–293. Springer, Cham (2016). https://doi.org/10.1007/978-3-319-46301-8_23
23. Sciancalepore, S., Oligeri, G., Di Pietro, R.: Strength of crowd (SOC)–defeating a reactive jammer in IoT with decoy messages. Sensors **18**(10), 3492 (2018). Special Issue on Emerging Methodologies and Practical Solutions for M2M and D2D Communications in the Internet of Things Era
24. Baktir, A.C., Ozgovde, A., Ersoy, C.: How can edge computing benefit from software-defined networking: a survey, use cases, and future directions. IEEE Commun. Surv. Tutor. **19**(4), 2359–2391 (2017, Fourthquarter)
25. Caprolu, M., Raponi, S., Di Pietro, R.: Fortress: an efficient and distributed firewall for stateful data plane SDN. Secur. Commun. Netw., 16 (2019)

Volunteer Cloud as an Edge Computing Enabler

Tessema M. Mengistu$^{(\boxtimes)}$, Abdullah Albuali, Abdulrahman Alahmadi,
and Dunren Che

Department of Computer Science, Southern Illinois University at Carbondale,
Carbondale, USA
{tessema.mengistu,aalbuali,aalahmadi,dche}@siu.edu

Abstract. The rapid increase in the number of devices connected to
the Internet, due to the Internet of Things, demands new ways of processing data produced by the devices. Edge Computing is one of the
solutions that tries to process data close to the origin, which is the edge
of networks. Emerging cloud systems, such as volunteer clouds, can also
be used towards the processing of data produced by IoT devices. This
paper proposes a Volunteer Computing as a Service (VCaaS) based Edge
Computing infrastructure. The paper addresses the architectural design
of the proposed system together with its research and technical challenges.

1 Introduction

The current computing landscape is entering a "post-cloud era" [5]. In this "post-
cloud-era", the major shift in the computing paradigm is due to the Internet of
Things (IoT), which is the digital interconnection of everyday objects with the
Internet [3]. This paradigm shift results in the explosion of devices connected to
the Internet that is estimated to reach 50 billion by 2020 [4]. These devices will
produce huge amount of data that need to be processed, stored, and transmitted
efficiently. IoT applications generally require a computing facility that can provide fast responses. So far, Cloud Computing data centers have been providing
the necessary computing infrastructures for the applications.

The data center based Cloud Computing infrastructures usually have a few
large data centers built in locations where construction and operational (e.g.
energy) costs are low [6]. As a result, these centralized data centers may be
located far away from the end users, resulting in higher round-trip network
latency. Due to the large geographical distances of the centralized data centers, processing data produced by IoT devices in public clouds entails some
challenges. These challenges create problems on the service quality of IoT applications in terms of delay, jitter, and throughput. Hence, the current centralized
cloud infrastructures will not suffice for IoT's network intensive applications
with very fast response requirements. One of the solutions to the above problem is moving the cloud infrastructure closer to users/devices by creating mini

© Springer Nature Switzerland AG 2019
T. Zhang et al. (Eds.): EDGE 2019, LNCS 11520, pp. 76–84, 2019.
https://doi.org/10.1007/978-3-030-23374-7_6

data centers or using devices at the edge of a network. This solution is called Edge/Fog Computing. The edge/fog proposal tries to create a middle layer cloud system so that part of the storage and computation can be done at the edge of a network instead of in the totality of the centralized cloud. Some of the advantages of Edge/Fog Computing include providing better Quality of Service (QoS) for delay-sensitive applications, such as video streaming, and reducing network communications and operational costs.

In the definition of Edge/Fog Computing, there is no standardized definition about the edge of a network and the devices that are expected to participate in the edge vary [7]. Vehicles, mobile base stations, networking devices, cloudlets, servers, smart phones etc., can all be part of Edge Computing. Volunteer computers at the edge of a network can also be used for Edge Computing. In this paper, we propose cloud infrastructures that are based on volunteer compute resources as a component in the Edge/Fog Computing fabric.

Volunteer cloud computing is an opportunistic cloud model that uses the spare donated resources of volunteer computers at the edge of a network to provide cheaper and greener cloud infrastructures and services [11]. Volunteer clouds come with multi-folds of benefits: no upfront investment for procuring a large number of servers; no maintenance costs such as electricity consumption for cooling and running the servers; boosting the utilization of computing resources (such as individually owned PCs). In the meantime, volunteer cloud computing introduces technical challenges that are centered on the high dynamics and high heterogeneity of volunteer computers. Moreover, volunteer computers are shared not only among cloud users but also between cloud users and local users of the machines. Novel and innovative algorithms and techniques that take the fundamental characteristics of volunteer computing in general and volunteer cloud computing in particular are needed to fully utilize the benefits. Volunteer cloud systems can not replace the powerful conventional data center based clouds, rather they complement those infrastructures.

Empirical evidences showed that volunteer clouds can be used to execute a range of applications [11,12]. Fault tolerant resource discovery and optimized VM placement techniques allow them to provide cloud services reliably and efficiently [9,10]. Moreover, the physical proximity of volunteer nodes to where applications originate, edge of networks, helps them in reducing the round-trip network latency of applications. However, since volunteer clouds depend on spare computing resources of less powerful computers, their overall computing capability may not suffice to handle highly resource intensive applications. As most applications naturally happen at the edge (of a network), volunteer clouds can be most conveniently deployed to directly serve these applications, edge applications, in cooperation with data center based conventional public clouds. Therefore, volunteer clouds are a perfect fit to the concept of Edge Computing.

This positional paper, elaborates on the concept of the usage of volunteer computing resources for Edge Computing. It discusses a high-level conceptual architecture of Volunteer Computing as a Service (VCaaS) based Edge Computing. Building upon our previous works, the following are the new contributions of this paper:

- It proposes the concept of the usage of volunteer cloud systems as a fabric in Edge Computing.
- It presents a high-level architecture of VCaaS based mini data centres as Edge Computing enablers.
- It explores technical and research challenges for the implementation of the VCaaS based Edge Computing.

The rest of the paper is organized as follows: Sect. 2 elaborates on the concept of volunteer cloud based Edge Computing together with its usage scenarios. Section 3 discusses the architecture of the proposed volunteer computing resources based Edge Computing. It also presents the technical and research challenges of implementing a fully-fledged VCaaS enabled Edge Computing infrastructure. Section 4 reviews related work and finally Sect. 5 concludes the paper and outlines future works.

2   Volunteer Cloud Computing as an Edge Computing Fabric

Currently, there are billions of Personal Computers (PCs) connected to the Internet [15]. Most of these computers are underutilized, usually used only for a few hours per day [14]. The usage of the aggregated spare compute resource of Personal Computers (PCs) to provide Cloud Computing services has been investigated [11]. Volunteer Computing as a Service (VCaaS) concept is proposed and implemented with encouraging performance results [11,12]. With novel and efficient resource management algorithms, reliable and efficient cloud services can be deployed over sporadically available PCs [9]. The VCaaS systems have the advantage of having a close proximity to where applications originate, the edge of a network. This physical proximity helps VCaaS systems to provide fast responses, context awareness, and more flexible mobility for applications. Moreover, VCaaS systems are cheaper and greener complements of the centralize data center based public clouds.

Contrary to the well-resourced data center based cloud systems, VCaaS systems depend on the scavenged spare compute resources of less powerful computers. This imposes a computing power limitation on VCaaS systems. This limitation can be off-setted by offloading computations to powerful public clouds, when the need arises. The cooperation of VCaaS systems with public cloud infrastructures and their proximity to the end users' applications help them to render edge services efficiently. The following motivational scenarios show how the proposed system can be used in real life situations.

University Campus Scenario: A student in a university campus wants to play an interactive game and she accessed the online game using the university's wifi. The public cloud provider that hosts the game detects the physical location of the customer and tries to initiates the offloading of the application to the nearby VCaaS system. Once the VCaaS system is identified, the public cloud can negotiate on issues such as pricing, QoS, etc., with the VCaaS system. After the negotiation concludes, the offloading of the application will be started. Once the offloading is completed the user will be redirected to the nearby VCaaS system that hosts the game. The offloaded instance will be cached or destroyed, when the user is done with playing. With this offloading, the user will get a better QoS from the application due to the reduced round-trip latency.

IoT Scenario: An air quality control research project uses sensors to collect environmental data and a public cloud infrastructure for data aggregation and processing. The project also uses a *credit-based* incentive model to encourage volunteers to use sensors on their smartphones and send the sensed data to the aggregation servers hosted on the public cloud. Volunteer users receive the credit they earned right after they send the data. The cloud provider that hosts the project sensed a surge of the volunteers' sensor data it receives for a particular day because of an advertisement about the project on a concert. In order not to lose the sensed data and respond to the new volunteer users as fast as possible, it uses the nearby VCaaS systems and allows the data to be received and aggregated by the infrastructures closer to the volunteers.

The two scenarios mentioned above give a glimpse of the usage of VCaaS systems as a middle layer in the Edge Computing paradigm. Some of the advantages of using VCaaS systems as a resource fabric in Edge Computing include:

- The significant reduction in the round-trip network latency due to the proximity of VCaaS systems to edge devices/applications. This reduction in the round-trip network latency will significantly improve the quality of experience of users and quality of service of applications, especially for time sensitive applications such as video streaming and interactive games.
- Complement the compute resources limitation of edge devices. Offloading is a mechanism where devices, such as smartphones, transfer the execution of a task to a centralized cloud partially or as a whole so as to conserve battery power or to leverage on the powerful compute resources of clouds. VCaaS systems can be an ideal choice for offloading tasks to complement computing resource limitations and to conserve battery for edge devices.
- Provision of context awareness and mobility to applications, as VCaaS systems are close to where data/applications originate.

3   Architecture of Volunteer Edge Computing

Considering the fact that the definition of Edge Computing is flexible on what constitute an "edge", we propose the inclusion of a collection of VCaaS systems as a component in the Edge Computing fabric. We propose a three layers architecture of VCaaS based volunteer edge computing composed of public cloud infrastructures (Public Cloud Layer), mini data center (VCaaS Layer), and front-end edge devices/applications (User Layer). The mini data center is a collection of volunteer cloud (VCaaS) systems. Each of the VCaaS systems bases its compute resource pool on the spare resources of computers within an organization/institution or homes. Figure 1 depicts the proposed three layers high-level architecture of the volunteer cloud based Edge Computing infrastructure.

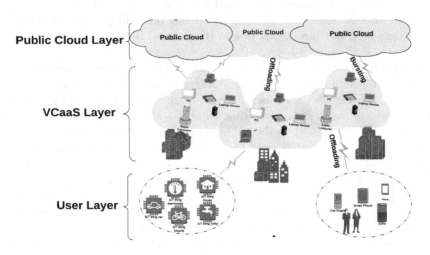

Fig. 1. High-level architecture of volunteer edge computing

Unlike cloud data centers, the mini data centers (VCaaS systems) are more diversified and resource constrained. This will create the need to exploit the computing capacities of remote public cloud services, such as Amazon EC2/S3, in case of increased compute resource requirements by the front-end edge devices/applications. Therefore, communication among the layers of the system can happen both vertically and/or horizontally.

– Vertical communication can happen between the layers through *offloading* and *bursting*. Offloading typically happens from resource-limited devices to a cloud to take advantage of the resource rich clouds or to conserve battery power. In our proposal, offloading can happen from the edge devices to the VCaaS systems. We also introduce an offloading from the public clouds to the VCaaS systems. This kind of offloading is mainly to exploit the proximity of the VCaaS systems to the edge devices/applications. Moreover, *bursting*, which is the offloading of excess load from private clouds to public clouds, is possible. The VCaaS systems can burst to the public clouds in the case of excess load.
– Horizontal communication in the middle layer, among the VCaaS systems is also possible. The VCaaS systems can create a form of loose federation in order to cater the computing and storage needs of applications at the edge of a network. The federation can be created dynamically according to the resource needs of edge devices/applications.

The implementation of this high-level architecture needs an extension at the Public Cloud Layer in such a way that it can discover suitable VCaaS(s) for offloading and managing issues such as QoS and contract management. Figure 2 depicts components at the Public Cloud and VCaaS layers.

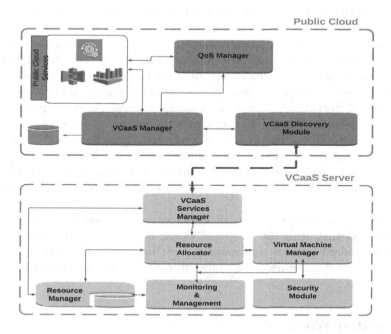

Fig. 2. Components of volunteer edge computing

As a blend of volunteer computing, cloud computing, mobile computing, and IoT, the volunteer edge computing proposal adopts both the challenges and opportunities of these systems and adds its own. There remain many open technical and research challenges for the full-fledged implementation of VCaaS based Edge Computing, the most notable ones being:

- Offloading and Partitioning:- Data/tasks can be offloaded from the edge devices to VCaaS systems to maximize on the donated compute resources and to conserve battery. Offloading can also happen from the public cloud to the VCaaS systems to leverage on the proximity of the VCaaS systems to the edge devices/applications in order to minimize network latency. Issues such as when to offload, what to offload, and how to offload are open issues that need to be investigated. Moreover, optimal ways of partitioning data/tasks for offloading should be researched.
- Communication Model:- Federation of clouds under the same and different providers has been researched in Cloud Computing context. In addition to this, the dynamic creation of clouds federation among VCaaS systems based on resource requests from User Layer should be investigated in VCaaS based edge computing. The volunteer edge computing should also define protocols and interfaces for both horizontal and vertical communications. Mechanisms

to select suitable VCaaS system(s) to offload data/application by the public cloud together with business model and QoS issues should also be investigated.

- Business Model:- Both Cloud and Volunteer Computing have their own business models, the first based on pay-as-you-go and the latter based on some incentives. The volunteer edge computing should device a business model that addresses how to handle offloading and bursting among the different layers of the architecture. This includes how to negotiate terms and prices of offloads (contract management) between the public cloud and VCaaS system.
- Quality of Service:- Volunteer Computing systems generally provide best effort services due to the intermittent availability and resource constraints of volunteer nodes as well as their non-intrusive characteristics [13]. This creates a problem to provide QoS guaranteed services by VCaaS systems. More research is needed towards providing quality guaranteed services in volunteer edge computing systems in order to increase their adoption for IoT applications.
- Security:- The security aspect of volunteer edge computing is complicated by the fact that using the untrusted VCaaS infrastructure base for potential cloud-standard business applications. New and innovative distributed security mechanisms are needed to fully utilize the potential of volunteer edge computing.

4   Related Work

The idea of using Edge Computing to cater the computational needs of IoT applications is intriguing. Prior works have exploited three types of hardware resources for computing on the edge: end devices, smart gateways, and local servers [8]. Volunteer edge/fog cloud computing systems that are based on donated spare resources of devices at the edge of the Internet are also proposed. Alonso-Monslave et al. proposed a public resource based fog computing. The proposal aims to use any type of device with Internet access and located at the edge of the network in order to deploy fog computing applications [1]. The authors used a simulator SimGrid to test performances using a video transfer system and claimed the reduction on the load of the cloud servers and better system performance. Nebula is a context and location aware distributed cloud infrastructure that uses volunteer edge resources [2]. An experimental set-up that emulates a volunteer platform using 50 PlanetLab nodes is used to test Nebula. The authors claimed that the deployed MapReduce tasks show superior performance improvement and better fault tolerance on Nebula. A deployment of fog computing by using participating devices, such as PCs, smartphones or smart TVs, at the edge of a network is studied in [1]. What makes our proposed system different from the above systems is that instead of using individual volunteer devices, we introduced a middle layer of federation of volunteer cloud systems that are based on volunteer compute resources.

5   Conclusion and Future Work

The rapid increase in the number of devices connected to the Internet, due to IoTs, demands new ways of processing data produced by the devices. Edge Computing is one of the solutions that tries to process the data close to the origin, the edge of networks. Volunteer computing resources can also be exploited to provide the necessary compute infrastructures for IoT devices/applications. In this paper we proposed and discussed a three layer Volunteer Computing as a Service based Edge Computing infrastructure. The volunteer edge computing architecture that we proposed is a blend of Volunteer Computing, Mobile Computing, IoT, and Cloud Computing. As future work, we plan to implement the proposed system using a VCaaS system that we have built in our lab called cuCloud. We also plan to conduct different performance evaluation experimentations for IoT and general applications using cuCloud as a middle layer in the proposed volunteer edge computing system.

References

1. Alonso-Monsalve, S., García-Carballeira, F., Calderón, A.: Fog computing through public-resource computing and storage. In: 2nd International Conference on Fog and Mobile Edge Computing (FMEC), pp. 81–87 (2017)
2. Ryden, M., Oh, K., Chandra, A., Weissman, J.: Nebula: distributed edge cloud for data-intensive computing. In: 2014 International Conference on Collaboration Technologies and Systems (CTS), pp. 491–492 (2014)
3. Conner, M.: Sensors empower the "Internet of things". EDN Netw. **55**, 32–37 (2010)
4. Evans, D.: The Internet of Things: how the next evolution of the Internet is changing everything, vol. 1, pp. 1–11. CISCO Internet Business Solutions Group (IBSG) (2011)
5. Shi, W., Dustdar, S.: The promise of edge computing. Computer **49**(5), 78–81 (2016)
6. Goiri, I., Le, K., Guitart, J., Torres, J., Bianchini, R.: Intelligent placement of datacenters for Internet services. In: 31st International Conference on Distributed Computing Systems, pp. 131–142 (2011)
7. Premsankar, G., Di Francesco, M., Taleb, T.: Edge computing for the internet of things: a case study. IEEE Internet Things J. **5**(2), 1275–1284 (2018)
8. Li, C., Xue, Y., Wang, J., Zhang, W., Li, T.: Edge-oriented computing paradigms: a survey on architecture design and system management. ACM J. Comput. Surv. **51**(2), 1–34 (2018). Quality of Service
9. Mengistu, T.M., Che, D., Alahmadi, A., Lu, S.: Semi-Markov process based reliability and availability prediction for volunteer cloud systems. In: 11th IEEE International Conference on Cloud Computing (2018 IEEE CLOUD), pp. 359–366 (2018)
10. Mengistu, T.M., Che, D., Lu, S.: Multi-objective resource mapping and allocation for volunteer cloud computing. In: 12th IEEE International Conference on Cloud Computing (2019 IEEE CLOUD), pp. 1–5 (2019)
11. Mengistu, T.M., Alahmadi, A.M., Alsenani, Y., Albuali, A., Che, D.: cuCloud: Volunteer Computing as a Service (VCaaS) system. In: Luo, M., Zhang, L.-J. (eds.) CLOUD 2018. LNCS, vol. 10967, pp. 251–264. Springer, Cham (2018). https://doi.org/10.1007/978-3-319-94295-7_17

12. Mengistu, T., Alahmadi, A., Albuali, A., Alsenani, Y., Che, D.: "No Data Center" solution to cloud computing. In: 10th IEEE International Conference on Cloud Computing (2017 IEEE CLOUD), pp. 714–717 (2017)

13. Mengistu, T.M., Che, D.: Survey and taxonomy of volunteer computing. ACM J. Comput. Surv. 1–35 (2019)

14. Domingues, P., Marques, P., Silva, L.: Resource usage of windows computer laboratories, pp. 469–476. IEEE (2005)

15. Gartner More than 1 Billion PCs In Use Worldwide and Headed to 2 Billion Units by 2014. http://www.gartner.com/newsroom/id/703807

Author Index

Alahmadi, Abdulrahman   76
Albuali, Abdullah   76

Badri, Hossein   31
Bahreini, Tayebeh   31

Caprolu, Maurantonio   59
Che, Dunren   76

Di Pietro, Roberto   59

George, Anjus   16
Grosu, Daniel   31

Kattiyan Ramamoorthy, Krishna Murthy   46

Menascé, Daniel A.   1
Mengistu, Tessema M.   76

Raponi, Simone   59
Ravindran, Arun   16

Sohraby, Kazem   46

Tadakamalla, Uma   1

Wang, Wei   46

Author Index

Printed in the United States
by Bookmasters

Printed in the United States
By Bookmasters